The Grind

living a "God-life" in the REAL WORLD

jeff edmondson and michael ross

Barefoot Ministries
Kansas City, Missouri

To Christopher, my son:
I love you, I'm proud of you, and I'll
never stop thanking God for you. I pray
that you'll always stay close to Him
during your journey.
—*Michael Ross*

To my boys, Logan and Brady:
You are my joy and life. I thank God for
the privilege of raising you. God's
blessings on your lives.
—*Jeff Edmondson*

Contents

It's Grind Time

Seventeen-year-old Kelly Price sat on the curb outside the youth room, scrunched into a ball, and facing the parking lot that had been transformed into a temporary skater's paradise. As often as she had watched her friends perform their tricks, she never got tired of it. She admired the amount of effort required to learn just one trick. Their dedication to their sport fascinated her.

Watching them skate was an escape, a retreat from all that life had dealt her. She had contemplated other means of escape, but none of those options were *really* options for her. While life for her was tough, unlike most of her friends, escape through drugs or alcohol was not really an escape. She had seen the results of these vices personally and she wanted no part of it. She was smart enough to know that those kinds of crutches became prisons in and of themselves.

Besides, she was a Christian. Or at least she felt like a Christian at times. Other times she didn't feel anything, like there was no difference between her and any other person who didn't claim Christianity. Now was one of those times. She felt like God was just letting her down.

Where is God? she wondered. *Why do I feel so numb?* If she couldn't rely on God, and escape by other means wasn't an option, what was she supposed to do?

Next to her sat her youth pastor, Kent, glued to the action in the makeshift skate park. For the longest time he said nothing. Kelly was glad of that. Just his presence alone was comforting to her. She was sure eventually he would say something, but for now she was glad to just have him there.

"Wow!" he exclaimed, finally breaking the silence. "That was impressive!" One of the skaters had just successfully ridden his skateboard the entire length of a raised steel pipe, crisply clearing the bottom edge and slapping all four wheels to the pavement below. "Love that trick."

"It's called a *grind*," Kelly said sarcastically.

Kent smiled and nodded. "Really? I wonder why they call it that?" he asked. Kelly knew he was baiting her. If there's one thing that Kent knew it was skating. His looks were deceiving. Though he didn't wear skater clothes, his hair was cut short, and despite the fact that he was at least a decade older than the oldest teen on the pavement, he could skate better than any of them. Kelly almost regretted making her comment now. But the silence had been broken, and frankly, she needed to talk.

"Well, possibly because as the skater rides the pipe it makes a grinding noise," Kelly stated. "Or possibly because when they ride the pipe, it grinds the edge of the skateboard down. Or maybe because if they fall off the pipe and plant their face into the pavement, their face gets ground into hamburger."

Kent looked at her, nodding with his eyebrows raised. "Possibly," Kent said. He let the silence fall between them again. Then after a good, long pause he said, "For some skaters learning how to grind a pipe is one of the most difficult tricks. It often gets the best of them and they just give up after a while."

"It would be cool if there was just a simple way to learn it, like flipping a switch or something," Kelly said.

Kent nodded. "Yeah, but if you don't have to work at it you would miss developing other skills along the way. Like the kind of balance it takes to pull off grinding the entire length of the pipe. Or how to kick-flip your board off a set of stairs."

"Still, wouldn't it be nice to just have it a little easier. What about all the spills the skater has to suffer through to get to that point? Lots of scrapes and bruises could be avoided, couldn't they?"

"It's part of the skateboarding experience," Kent said. "Each bruise is a lesson learned. You choose whether to grow from it, to learn from it, or to let it defeat you." Kelly knew he was speaking metaphorically now. Pastor Kent had a gift for taking everyday occurrences and turning them into life lessons. She thought for a moment.

"OK, how long does it take to learn a new trick?" she asked.

"Depends on the person," Kent said. "Some can get it in a week. Most times a lot longer. But with steady practice and someone to keep an eye on form and technique, a skater should be able to land a trick in four weeks."

Kelly considered his words and silence fell between them again. A couple of skaters tried unsuccessfully to ride the pipe, each landing hard on the concrete. Despite their failures, they both got up and kept trying.

Kent finally spoke. "So, Kelly, a month ago I challenged you with a daily Bible reading plan. How's that going for you?"

Kelly had known the question was going to come eventually. She shrugged. "Not so good," she said. "Can't say I've thumbed through the pages much in the last month."

Kent smiled knowingly. "You know, life is a lot like that steel pipe. At first glance it looks cold and harsh, but with some time, some practice, and some scrapes and bruises you can learn to rise above it. Life can sometimes grind you down. It will send you headlong into the pavement if you don't learn how to cope with it in a healthy, uplifting manner. Best way I know how to cope with it is through the Bible."

Kelly considered his words. She'd had similar conversations with him in the past. But somehow this time it made sense. Maybe it was the reality of grinding the pipe that made it seem more real. Maybe it was just the right timing. She couldn't put her finger on it, but somehow she knew he was right. She really hadn't given God the chance to work in her life, to bring answers to the questions that plagued her. But she had to give it a shot if she was going to get through this difficult time.

"A month to land a trick on a board?" she asked.

"Yep, a month's work can usually change some things considerably" Kent said smiling.

"So me not reading the Bible like you said, is kind of like looking at the pipe and just walking away" Kelly said, intuitively.

"You know, I didn't think of that, but I guess it does work kind of the same way." he said, playing dumb as best he could.

Just at that moment one of the skater's popped the board onto the steel rail and skidded down it gracefully, glancing the end and planting two feet and four wheels to the concrete in perpetual motion.

She was ready. She was tired of focusing on the cold and harsh. She was prepared to put in the time. She was ready for *the grind!*

* * * * *

Feeling a little like Kelly? Maybe it's time to examine your relationship with God. Start by taking the quiz that follows.

Quiet-Time Quiz

Mark the responses that apply to you. Be honest!

____ I often find myself more concerned with hanging out with the popular crowd, getting noticed by the opposite sex, and keeping up with the latest trends than with spending time alone with God.

____ Prayer is something I only do at the dinner table and/or at church.
____ I spend very little time reading the Bible because I have a hard time understanding how it applies to my life.
____ Due to my busy schedule, I find it difficult to make room in my day for "quiet time" with God.
____ God seems far away.

The 28-Day Experiment: Steps to Success

There's much more to a Christian teen's life than food, friends, and fun. It's time to plug your life into the one and only power Source—Jesus.

We know what you're thinking: Sounds good, but how? After all, your life feels like a roller coaster sometimes, right? One minute you're on a giant spiritual high, usually after hearing a great speaker or returning from camp or a short-term mission trip. But give it a week, maybe two, and crash! The spiritual high often takes a hike along with a bunch of other commitments and promises you made.

So how can you keep that mountain high even when your feet are stuck in the real world? And what are the steps to standing firm spiritually when pressure makes you squirm?

Step 1: Feed the fire. The flame that was sparked at camp will fizzle if it's not fueled regularly. So what should you do? Spend time every day (even if it's just 10 to 15 minutes) reading Scripture, along with the daily readings in this book.

Step 2: Pray. Don't just "do your duty" with canned, programmed expressions that sound nice, or empty words that really don't reflect your heart. Spend a quiet time with Jesus every day, thinking about His Word (Bible verses), telling Him of your love and devotion, and talking to Him about others and their needs (as well as your own). In any relationship, two-way communication is vital.

Step 3: Be Accountable. Find a couple of trustworthy Christian friends and form an accountability group. Ask these guys or girls to help you stick to the commitments you made during the summer. Meet together or talk on the phone at least once a week.

Read *The Grind* and follow our devotional plan for 28 days straight—especially after returning from camp or a mission trip. Don't be surprised if you see a change in your spiritual life.

How Do I Live the "God-Life" in the Real World?

Each section begins with **Tales from the Grind**. These comics take a close look at the struggles in developing a consistent relationship with God. Read these stories and think of ways that the characters are similar or different from you.

Next, complete the **Wake-Up Call** Bible study at the beginning of each week. These are designed to help you apply scripture to your life and to prepare you for the daily devotionals.

Daily Devotionals

Set aside time each day to develop a deeper relationship with God. Each daily devotional contains:

● **"Tales from the Grind"**—A story taken from "real life."

● **Think About It!** This will help you begin to center your mind on the theme for that day.

● **Feed Your Face.** This is the focus scriptures for that day. These passages will help explore how God's Word speaks to the topic for that devotion.

● **180.** You will discover ways to live out your Christian faith in the "daily grind" of life.

Here's a brief overview of each section:

Section 1: What Tag Do You Wear?

You'll learn what it really means to wear the tag "Christian" and why a knockout body and popularity won't fulfill you. Plus, we give you an action plan that will help you align your goals with God, prepare for hand-to-hand combat, and save the world through radical Christianity.

Topics covered: commitment, mind-set, choices, values, authentic faith, temptation, sin.

Section 2: Working on Your Walk

This section tackles God's plan of salvation, why Christ died on the Cross, tips on prayer, how to be completely sold out to the Savior, and how to be a light in the darkness of the real world.

Topics covered: religion vs. Christianity, religion vs. relationship, prayer, the Word, spiritual responsibility, humble service, sacrifice.

Section 3: Righteous Relationships

"A good friend is . . ." and "A good friend isn't . . ." We give strategies for relationship building, detailing the fine art of being a good friend.

Topics covered: peer groups, peer pressure, put-downs, dating, sex, peer evangelism, loyalty.

Section 4: Life at Home

Communication, understanding, and respect: keys to surviving at home (and to resolving those Tuesday night fights).

Topics covered: family life, changing families, hassles, independence, listening, communication, family fights.

Tales from the *Grind*

Burned o

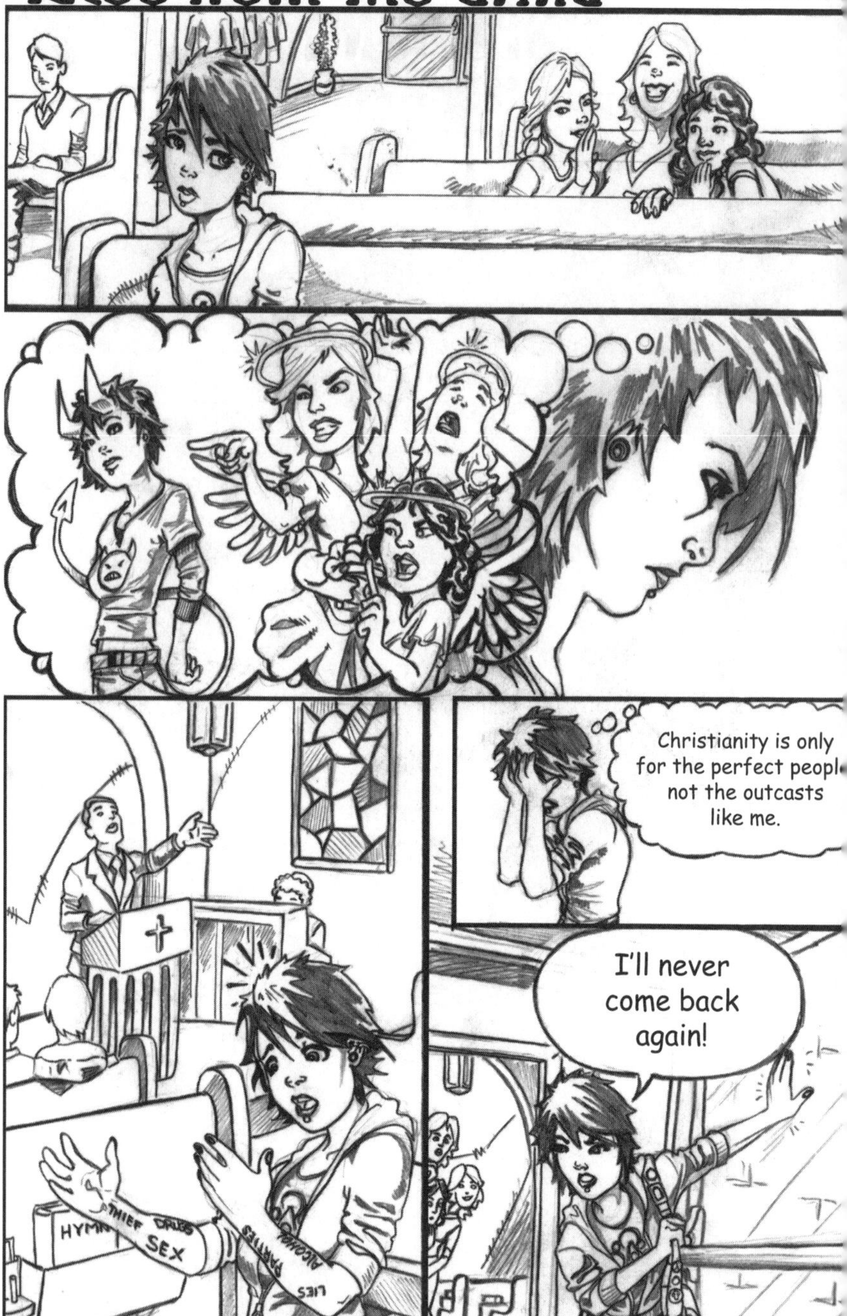

SECTION 1
WHAT TAG DO YOU WEAR?

Enough Is Enough!

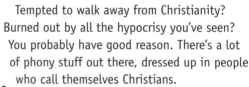

Wake-Up Call

Weekly Bible Study

Tempted to walk away from Christianity? Burned out by all the hypocrisy you've seen? You probably have good reason. There's a lot of phony stuff out there, dressed up in people who call themselves Christians.

But if you're gauging Christianity by the actions of others, you'll always be disappointed. The truth is that nobody is perfect—not even the most committed believers in your youth group.

Does this mean that all those who claim to be Christians are a bunch of hypocrites? No, just human. Nobody will ever achieve perfection in this life. But with the help of the Holy Spirit, you can be transformed into the image of the One who has a perfect relationship with God—Jesus Christ.

So before we dig in, let's make a pact with each other: Starting today, I'll get my eyes off everyone else and put my focus on Jesus.

* * *

Take a few minutes to complete the activities below:

● List the top 10 role models of your generation.

1. ....

2. ....

3. ....

4. ....

5. ....

6. ....

7. ....

8. ....

9. ....

10. ....

For each person you listed, answer these two questions:
Why do people consider this person a role model?
What are this person's good and/or bad qualities?

● Name some role models who have "fallen from grace."

Here are a few to get you started: Britney Spears, Michael Vick, and Lindsay Lohan.

Despite the mistakes humans often make, we can always count on and look up to the ultimate role model—Jesus Christ. He was never brought down by sin and never will be. Are you searching for the perfect role model? All you have to do is look to Christ!

● Read John 5:39-40.

The Jewish priests in this passage—men who had committed their lives to studying Scripture and to seeking the Messiah—met Jesus face-to-face and yet rejected Him. Imagine that! They distrusted the Messiah because He didn't fit their human definition of how the ultimate role model should look and behave.

● Read the following scriptures, and then jot down your impressions of Jesus.

John 15:13-17

Matt. 9:35-36

Col. 1:13-20

Rev. 3:20-22

John 1:32-36

If Jesus is truly everything you just described, wouldn't it be great to get to know Him even better? (We mean really get to know Him in a deep, intimate, growing relationship.) Good—we're glad you nodded your head yes because that's what this Bible study (and book) is all about.

Let's go deeper:

● Write your definition of "true Christianity":
(Hint: Jesus is the foundation.)

● Read Phil. 2:8; then read Rom. 6:9-11.

In what way do we also "die"? What responsibility do we have in our "deaths"? (Read Rom. 6:11-14 for a giant hint.)

Just as Jesus died because of His love for His Heavenly Father, we must do likewise. This means giving up everything for Christ. It also means putting Him first and obeying Him. If you haven't already noticed, this can be hard.

But here's some really cool news: When we give up our lives to Christ, He gives them back to us fuller, stronger, and better than before. He rewards us with new dreams, new desires, and an awesome new future. And here's some even cooler news: If we let Him, Jesus helps us to step out of our old lives and to step into the new one He has planned for us.

● So what are your dreams? Don't limit yourself. Jot down everything that's in your heart.

Short-range dreams

....

....

....

....

....

Long-range dreams

....

....

....

....

....

Take a long, hard look at your list, and try to imagine how you can serve God as He helps you to fulfill these dreams.

● Read Jer. 29:11-13.

How do you discover God's plans for your life? (Hint: Commit your life, your will, everything to Jesus, and you'll gradually learn what He has in mind for you.)

● Read Heb. 12:1-3.

Now would be a good time to pray. Talk to God about what you've learned in this study, and ask Him to reveal areas of your life that need work (sins to confess, habits to overcome, desires to commit to Him).

Ask Jesus to help you "die" to the life you once lived and to move ahead on solid ground with Him.

During the next few days, take some time to dream about what the supreme future would be like. Each time a cool idea hits you, add it to your list. Next, talk to your parents, coach, teacher, or youth leader about what it will take to achieve some of the ideas on your dream list.

Day 1: Commitment
Make Them Thirsty

*You are the salt of the earth. But if the salt loses its saltiness . . .
it is no longer good for anything (Matt. 5:13).*

Jason can't sleep. His mind is racing full speed with haunting scenes from the day.

Ever since committing his life to Jesus at youth retreat, Jason has been under pressure from the other guys on the football team.

"Man, you're insane!"

"Jason's gone religious on us."

"What? You're some kind of Christian?"

Jason stares at the Bible on his bedside table. It looks so odd just sitting there. He thinks of the youth meeting coming up next week (and his pledge to say a few words to the group). *What have I done?* he wonders. *What am I going to do?*

Think About It!

Ever notice how everyone at school is squeezed into a category of some kind? Jock, cheerleader, geek, punk, goth, skater, Jesus freak. It's almost as if everyone runs around campus wearing an invisible sign. And you know what happens if you don't fall into the so-called right category: Life can be miserable.

But as a Christian, you should get your identity from God's Word—not from what sport you play, the crowd you hang out with, or your hairstyle. If you want to make a difference in this world, you must realize that you are "the salt of the earth." If you live a life that is salty, you will eventually make people thirsty for what you have. On the other hand, if you forget your identity, you may "lose your saltiness," losing your effectiveness in spreading His Word. And the worst way to ruin your witness is by being ashamed of your faith and melting into a phony Christian.

There's One in whom you'll never see an ounce of hypocrisy. His name is Jesus Christ. Look at Him. Read about Him. Serve Him. Study Him. You'll never find anything in Him that will cause you to stumble. Jesus Christ is genuine Christianity personified, and He's your standard of who to be and how to act.

Explore these scriptures:

Feed Your Face

Luke 9:23-27

Eph. 2:1-7

Col. 3:12-17

When Jesus was on earth, He encountered many religious phonies. He called them "whitewashed tombs, which look beautiful on the outside but on the inside are full of dead men's bones" (Matt. 23:27). There's comfort in knowing that you're not the only one who experiences hypocrisy. The Lord notices it too.

If you are feeling like a fake in some area of your life, God is trying to get your attention. Listen to Him. God loves His children, but He hates hypocrisy. Admit your phoniness to Him, and He'll forgive you. Just tell Him about it. Tell Him you want to be genuine like His Son. Remember this: "If we confess our sins, he is faithful and just and will forgive us our sins and purify us from all unrighteousness" (1 John 1:9). Confess your hypocrisy as often as you sense its presence. The Bible's truth never wears out.

Living a genuine Christian life is not your job alone. The Holy Spirit will help you. Learn to relax in the shade of this verse: "I have been crucified with Christ and I no longer live, but Christ lives in me"

21

(Gal. 2:20). The more you look at Him, the more you find that He lives His life through you. Sound confusing? Don't worry. Keep looking at Christ. With time, He'll teach you the truth of Gal. 2:20. And as that happens, the result will be real, not fake like your past weak attempts at being a "good Christian."

Day 2: Mind-set
Are You "Cross-eyed"?

If anyone would come after me, he must deny himself and take up his cross and follow me (Matt. 16:24).

Jennifer's face flushes when Brandon surprises her with a long kiss—right on the lips. She pulls back and awkwardly fumbles through her purse, acting as if she is looking for something.

"What's wrong?" Brandon asks. "It was just a kiss. Don't be so uptight."

"Look, I just don't want an audience, OK?" Jennifer says, pointing to her parents' bedroom window. "Mom and Dad are still up."

"Then let's leave," he says. "You don't have to be home till 11, and it's only 10:15. We're early."

Brandon leans against the steering wheel and looks at her with those gorgeous blue eyes. "We could drive to the lake, find a private place, and you know . . . make out."

Jennifer sits there—completely stunned. She knew Brandon from youth group and was excited when he finally asked her out. But he suddenly seemed too pushy.

It's only our first date, and he wants to make out! Jennifer tells herself. *This is just wrong—especially for Christians. But if I don't go with him, it'll be social suicide with my friends. Everybody will think I'm weird. What should I do God?*

Then Jennifer thinks about the cross hanging around her neck and the commitment she made to Jesus. She opens the car door, steps out, and turns to Brandon.

"You're a great guy, and I had a good time, but the fun stops here. Later."

Think About It!

Sometimes living up to the title "Christian" and stepping out as a godly guy or girl can feel like the world's most impossible task.

No one wants to be rejected. So in the face of sneers, smirks, and rolling eyes, you tell yourself, *I gotta look cool. I'll just go along with the group.* Before you know it, you take your eyes off Jesus and begin to compromise in subtle ways—through your thoughts, your attitudes, your conversations, your relationships—and wham! you suddenly find yourself acting anything but godly.

What you really need is rock-solid security—something that hangs in there even when everything else in your life comes crashing down around you.

There's only one place to look—the Cross.

Explore these scriptures:

Feed Your Face

Exod. 20:1-20

John 15:18-27

1 Cor. 1:18-25

Commit to being "Cross-eyed." Ask God to tear down idols in your life—a relationship, a job, a possession—anything you value more than Him. Is there something you need to confess to God? This is the crucial first step to gaining a deeper, righteous walk with the Lord.

Take the triple W challenge. Be 100 percent sold out to the worship of God, the work of God, and the Word of God.

Keep your appointments with Jesus. Relationships can be good only when there is close communication. That means talking to Jesus and listening. Make an effort to spend time alone with Him every day, praising and thanking Him, telling Him about the needs of others as well as your own.

Set your mind on the Word. God gave us the Bible and a whole sup-
ply of standards to live by. Anybody can give you a new set of rules. But
God gives you the best reason of all: life—incredible, abundant, eternal
life. He wants the very best for you. His plans for you are even better
than your wildest dreams.

Day 3: Choices
A Decision Can Last a Lifetime

The Lord watches over the way of the righteous, but the way of the wicked will perish (Ps. 1:6).

Jason is invited by a friend to attend a party. When Jason walks to the backyard of the house where the party is held, he realizes that it is more than just a get-together. He is about to leave when his friend comes up to him and offers him a beer. Jason's mind is flooded with thoughts:

What will my friends think?
What should I do?
I've never done anything like this before.
Will God forgive me?
But everybody else is doing it.
It must be OK.
I guess there's nothing wrong with it.
I'll just do it once.
How loaded can I get from just one?
This isn't really good for me.
Nobody will accept me if I say no.
How will I get home if I'm wasted?
How wasted can I get from just one?
Why am I doing this?
What will they say if I turn them down?
Maybe I ought to leave. What would happen if I left?
What's the big deal? It's not like I'll get hooked.
I gotta decide. Gotta decide now.
What should I do?

Think About It! **Decisions. Every day you're forced to make hundreds of them:** split-second choices, decisions that can blow up in your face and change your life forever—or even end it. It's no wonder you feel so much pressure!

It's so easy to let your emotions lead you around by the nose, or to just follow the crowd when the pressure gets tough. But the truth is that it doesn't matter if somebody pushed you into that choice or you just had to react too fast. If you make the wrong decision, you go down—hard. What's more, you end up having to deal with the consequences.

And that's the problem with going along with the group and allowing other people to make your choices. You're not living your life anymore. They are. And when it comes time to pay the price, you end up doing it all by yourself.

Christians—we mean the authentic, 100 percent, rock-solid, sold-out kind—have learned how to make the right choices when the pressure is on or off.

Explore these scriptures:

Feed Your Face

2 Chron. 15:1-15

Matt. 25:14-30

Rom. 7:14-25

Take responsibility for your actions. What it all comes down to is this: You have to call the shots for yourself and take responsibility for what happens whether you like it or not.

Know what you believe. Build a set of values right now and think about your actions before you get into a tight spot. Weigh the consequences of your decisions before you act, and find the hidden dangers before they sneak up on you. This is one of the best defenses you can develop. By preplanning your response and having your values thought out beforehand, you are more prepared to act as you want to act—not as the group wants you to act.

Seek Christian friends who share your values. And spend less time with friends who aren't interested in pursuing a godly walk. Like it or not, the people you spend time with have a big influence on your life. If your pals are doing things you know are wrong, don't let them drag you down too. You might even consider not hanging out with them.

Day 4: Values

Who's Right?

The way of the LORD is a refuge for the righteous, but it is the ruin of those who do evil (Prov. 10:29).

"Don't give me that!" Jennifer said to Brandon. "You're saying you don't agree with it only because that's what you've always heard from your parents. What's really wrong with it?"

Brandon stared uncomfortably at his date. He was blown away by her comment and didn't know how to respond. A minute ago they were talking about a friend who had gotten pregnant. Suddenly the conversation exploded into a heated debate over abortion.

What do I believe? he wondered. *Am I just repeating what I've always heard?*

Brandon's stomach rumbled impatiently.

Where'd the waitress disappear to anyway? If he and Jennifer could order some food, maybe they could get off the subject—and have a peaceful evening.

"Don't you have a response?" Jennifer insisted.

Brandon paused for a moment. One night at youth group a guest speaker had come and clicked through grisly slides of what really happens during an abortion. He remembered feeling sick to his stomach when he saw pictures of the actual aborted babies.

How could any country be so shameless as to legalize the murder of innocent children? he remembered thinking to himself.

Brandon spoke up. "Look, I believe abortion is wrong," he said. "My parents may have influenced me, but I make my own decisions. And I think it's sad that you actually believe abortion is simply a matter of choice. I bet an unborn child would disagree with you."

29

Think About It!

Ever been in Brandon's shoes? Have you ever been called out on your beliefs?

We live in an age when moral issues have been so clouded by a zillion different opinions that it's often hard to distinguish between right and wrong—even for Christians.

For example, most Christian teens would agree that stealing is wrong, but how about copying your friend's homework assignment? Is that wrong? Is it OK to "borrow" $5 from your little brother's piggy bank without telling him—returning it later? Is it really wrong to tell Mom and Dad you're going to a friend's house when in reality you're just meeting there to head off to a party?

Regardless of what you hear at school or what the entertainment industry says, understand that God wants to help you make right choices for everything in life. Truth does exist—and Jesus Christ is the foundation. In fact, God has a definite set of values He wants us to follow. The cool thing is that He didn't leave us in the dark. There is this book called the Bible, and it sets out the blueprints for a life lived for God. By digging into God's Guidebook and by spending time with Him, you'll learn right from wrong.

Explore these scriptures:

Feed Your Face

Matt. 22:15-38

Phil. 4:4-8

James 1:16-25

Discover God's way of doing things. Admit to God that you don't have all the answers. But let Him know that you want to do the right thing. God is faithful to point out what's right and wrong in life.

Share your struggle. Sometimes we don't like the answers God gives us. When you feel this way, talk to a Christian adult you trust. Sometimes talking things out helps you to accept the truth. Besides, having someone else share your struggle is better than going it alone.

Make your stand. Never be afraid to speak up and tell others what you know is right. Someone else may be searching for answers on an issue you've settled. If that person asks, you owe it to him or her to share what God has told you.

Day 5: Authentic Faith
Wide-eyed Innocence

Now faith is being sure of what we hope for and certain of
what we do not see (Heb. 11:1).

It wasn't something you ever thought much about. It just happened.

They said it would happen every day, and it did. Sometimes in the mornings, sometimes in the evenings, but mostly in the afternoons. During the rainy season in the country of Panama, a rain shower would hit daily.

And for an active kid like Brett rain was worse than the dentist's drill—unless, of course, you learned to deal with it. Since Brett had no choice and since he's an optimist, he made the best of it.

One day Brett rummaged through Dad's junk woodpile until he found the perfect board. Then his sister helped him cut, seal, and paint it. The two concocted a ditch speedboat—ideal for racing in the flooded ditches near Albrook Air Force Base.

The next day the two went outside and waited with wide-eyed innocence. They hadn't checked the weather forecast. They hadn't asked their parents if it was going to rain. They simply waited and believed it would happen.

Without fail, the clouds gathered and the sky darkened. Soon a torrential downpour pounded the earth—just as it had every day during the rainy season. As strong currents of water moved through the ditches, the speedboat race kicked into action, lasting all afternoon.

Think About It!

Wide-eyed innocence. Believing in something even when you don't understand it. Trusting with your whole heart. Through the years we've learned that these are the ingredients of authentic faith.

We would love to revisit those early days of our lives. Even as adults, we crawl out of bed some mornings and find it hard to have faith in anything—especially faith that we're Christians. We feel rotten sometimes. We get mad. We struggle with Bible studies and prayer times. Being a Christian is supposed to be easier than this, right?

In a word, no!

As Christians, God has forgiven our sins and has given us new lives through Jesus Christ. But He didn't promise that everything would go smoothly or that we'd always feel 100 percent thrilled about being Christians.

Yet we've learned that becoming a strong, authentic Christian comes only when we allow God the time to deepen our faith—regardless of how we feel. And it's the same for you. So get it into your head right now that you can trust God 100 percent. Just as it never fails to rain during Panama's wet season, God never goes back on any of His promises. Sometimes it just takes a little while to realize it.

Explore these scriptures:

Feed Your Face

Ps. 13

Matt. 8:1-13

James 2:14-24

Make up your mind. Despite the fact that you don't feel like a Christian sometimes, don't let your emotions play head games with you. If you are working on your relationship with Jesus—striving to obey Him—you can rest assured that you are a Christian. All relationships go through an ebb and flow. If your walk with Jesus is dry, take inventory on your faith. Ask yourself a couple of questions: Am I doing something to hinder my relationship with Jesus? Do I need to ask God for forgiveness for sins I've committed?

Ask for help. If you're having spiritual problems, ask Jesus to give you a boost. Don't just ask once and then forget about it. Keep asking. Then wait and see what happens. Have faith. The rain will come; we promise.

Day 6: Temptation

Fight, Flight, or Fright— You Choose

Therefore put on the full armor of God, so that when the day of evil comes, you may be able to stand your ground, and after you have done everything, to stand (Eph. 6:13).

Gina was tempted to do it.

What she wanted desperately was on the desk in front of her, within her grasp. The answers to tomorrow's American Literature final exam could be hers for the taking. Mrs. Ray, her teacher, had stepped out of the room for about 10 minutes. Gina had been left alone.

Mrs. Ray had invited Gina to stop by the class after school to work on an extra credit essay. With an F as her grade that semester, Gina needed all the help she could get. But this was way too easy!

This could solve my problems, she told herself, keeping an eye on the door. *But it would be cheating. Yet I did pray this morning, asking the Lord to help me pass this class. Could God have set up this whole thing?*

It was Gina's senior year, and she didn't want anything to keep her from graduating. Yet cheating didn't sound the least bit appealing. Deep inside, she knew it would be wrong. She also knew that God would have no part in it. Still, the thought of being held back from graduating stabbed at her insides.

I could just jot down a couple of answers instead of the whole thing. I'll never get another chance like this. What should I do?

Just as Gina was about to scribble the first answer onto a note pad, the door opened.

"Hey, Gina," her teacher said with a smile. "So how's the essay coming along?"

"Oh, uh—great!" Gina said, her face turning bright red. "Thanks again, Mrs. Ray. I mean, thanks for giving me a chance to score some extra points—you know, with the essay and all."

"Of course, Gina," Mrs. Ray said. "I don't want you to fail. Look, give me some honest effort with this essay, and I'll give you a passing grade."

Gina was stunned. She slumped down in her seat.

Lord, I am so sorry, she prayed silently. I nearly cheated—and blew my one chance to pass this class—the chance I know now that You gave me. Please forgive me.

Think About It!

Gina was fortunate this time. But if she doesn't learn how to withstand temptation in the future, she could end up on a collision course with disaster.

You see, Satan uses temptation to convince us of doing something we know is wrong. His goal is to pull us as far as possible away from God. And Satan will do anything to get us to give in, especially if it means convincing us that God wants us to give in. Before we know it, we regret taking our eyes off God.

But don't be confused. Temptation in itself is not sin. Jesus was tempted yet never sinned. It's what you do after you are tempted that determines whether or not you sin.

Here's a scary fact: You'll never escape temptation—on this side of heaven, that is. Regardless of how deep you grow as a Christian, temptation will be a part of life. But here's some good news: The stronger you grow in Christ, the easier it gets to withstand temptation.

Basically, there are three ways of responding to temptation:

Giving in *(which isn't an option for Christians)*
Running *(which is sometimes your only choice)*
Waging a battle *(which is usually your best choice)*

So why is the third option usually the best option? Because it involves relying on the Holy Spirit and confronting evil with the truth. This is exactly what Jesus did when He was tempted in the desert (see Matt. 4:1-11).

In other words, when Gina spotted the test answers on her teacher's desk and when temptation set in, her best option would have been to stand firm in the truth of Christ and pray, *"Jesus, Your Word states that cheating is a sin. I know it's wrong. Please help me to withstand this temptation."*

Explore these scriptures:

Feed Your Face

Eph. 6:10-18

1 Cor. 10:11-13

James 1:12-16

Become a fighter. Realize that Satan has no power over you, and don't let him fool you into thinking he does. With this knowledge, it's easier to allow the Holy Spirit to help you fight back when you face temptation.

Fight fire with power! God has provided scriptures that provide power in our battle with evil. It's what Jesus beat Satan with in the desert, and it's available for you to use as well (again, see Matt. 4:1-11). Also, begin memorizing scripture that will help you be strong when you need it.

Seek help from other Christians. Just as we suggested at the beginning of this book, find an accountability partner and meet regularly with this person. Knowing that someone is going to ask if you've slipped in an area of your life is often enough of a deterrent against giving in to temptation.

Day 7: Sin

The Dark Side

*I tell you the truth, everyone who sins is a slave to sin
(John 8:34).*

Jeremy thought he'd stumbled upon a gold mine. While using his older brother's computer, he'd come across a stash of hidden files on the hard drive. But this file wasn't filled with documents or spreadsheets. It was packed with incredible photos of air-brushed fantasies.

Oh man, wait till the guys hear about this! Jeremy thought. He knew all about online porn. His parents had lectured him about the dangers of the online community, and his computer was protected by smart filters that prevented him from being able to access such sites or download objectionable material. But apparently his brother had online access that far exceeded his parents' awareness. Jeremy had never imagined how graphic they were. Jeremy was mesmerized by the vivid images adorning the screen. Each photo fueled all kinds of weird feelings deep inside of him. Only yesterday, Jeremy had gone out of his way to avoid the girls at his old school. After all, they *had* threatened to wipe out every boy with the dreaded disease known as cooties. But now, at fourteen, females seemed much more grown-up—much more fascinating.

Suddenly the bedroom door burst open and a sharp voice ripped through the silence.

"You little runt!" screamed his big brother, Kevin. "Get outta my room! How dare you snoop through my computer?"

"Kevin, come on, man. Why didn't you show me this stuff?"

"Because it's not for nosey, little kids, like you!" Kevin shouted, pushing Jeremy out of the way.

"I'm 14, Kevin! I know about sex."

Kevin scrambled to begin closing the files that Jeremy had opened on the desktop. He had a large collection of photos. "How'd you get past mom and dad's smart filters to get those?" Jeremy asked.

"Who says I got past the filters? You don't have to surf the net to get access to this kind of stuff." Kevin continued to close down files as quickly as his index finger could click. "I have friends who have access and I have an e-mail address. Why do *I* need to go surfing? It comes to me."

Jeremy nodded. He'd never thought of that. "Yeah, that would work," he replied thinking. "Don't you feel guilt looking at that stuff, sometimes?"

"Shut up!" snapped Kevin, closing down the last file—then he shoved Jeremy out the bedroom door.

Jeremy stood in the hall, this strange curiosity burned inside of him and slowly mixed with fear and confusion. *Lord, what have I done?*

Think About It! **How can life get so messed up anyway?** Why is it so hard to make good choices?

Sin takes what God created and distorts it. For example; it takes a beautiful God-created thing like sex—intended to be shared between two people who love each other within the marriage relationship—and distorts it into something perverted, like pornography. Sin blinds our eyes to the truth and enslaves those who believe its lies.

God came to us in the form of a Man—Jesus Christ (God in the flesh). He actually came to earth; walked like us, talked like us, laughed and cried like us, and then suffered and died on a cross so that all our sins could be forgiven. He came that we may have a life free from the bondage of sin. All we have to do is say no to all the bad choices that come our way, put our trust in Him, and truly believe that He will provide.

Sin is a choice. When you compare what you have to choose from (earthly stuff) with what God wants to give you (abundant life), it just doesn't stand up. And as a Christian, you don't have to think so much about what you're saying no to—because what you're saying yes to is so much better.

Explore these scriptures:

Feed Your Face

Rom. 6:1-14

Rom. 7:7-25

Rom. 8:1-17

Guard your mind. The Bible warns us not to tempt ourselves and not to be conformed to the garbage the world offers us. In other words, stay far away from such evil—those things that go against. The Lord wants us to become imitators of God and to fill our minds with "whatever is true, whatever is noble, whatever is right, whatever is pure, whatever is lovely, whatever is admirable" (Phil. 4:8).

Remember: Temptation isn't sin . . . yet. There's a big difference between temptation and sin. We're all tempted, but we don't have to sin. James 1:12 says, "Blessed is the man who perseveres under trial, because when he has stood the test, he will receive the crown of life that God has promised to those who love him."

Accept God's forgiveness. He loves you and will welcome you back into His arms if you've failed. But you can't be fake. You have to truly desire to change and to follow Him. (This is called repentance.)

39

Tales from the *Grind*

Wake~Up Call

Weekly Bible Study

Is It OK to Have Questions?

Questions. Everyone has questions concerning Christianity. Even believers who accepted Christ years ago still have questions. Some of those questions will never be answered until we stand face-to-face with Jesus. Others can be answered fairly easily. In this section we'll attempt to wipe out a few of those nagging questions that need to be answered in order for you to grow spiritually. Want a quick overview of what this week's got in store?

Here are a few of the questions we'll tackle:

I've had enough religion. Isn't there something better?

How can my life have true meaning?

OK, I've accepted Jesus. What now?

How do I find out what God wants?

● Got Questions?

I'm a Christian. I attend church regularly. I've accepted Jesus as my Savior. I went to the altar and "prayed through." It was a great experience, but I've never really recaptured that feeling ever since. Honestly, after that night I didn't know what to do. I've got a Bible, and I knew I should read it. I just didn't know where to start. I'm not even sure I know what Jesus did for me. I feel like I'm floundering. What should I do?

A lot of people who become Christians suffer from the same problems. They just don't know what to do. Let's start our study by finding out who Jesus really is. Do you have your Bible and a sharp pencil? Find and read the following passages. In the space provided, rewrite in your own words what the scripture says:

41

Luke 1:26-38

Matt. 1:18-25

Mark 1:9-12

Rom. 1:3-4

Jesus is the Son of God. He became flesh through a miraculous pregnancy in order to provide a far greater miracle later on.

OK, so Jesus is God's Son. I knew that already. I also know He died for me. But what's that really mean?

Stay with us. You know Jesus died for you. It's important to establish that fact before we go any further. Write down below your best guess as to why you think He did it:

Now let's see how close you are to being correct. Read the following:
John 15:12-14
Rom. 5:6-8
1 Pet. 3:18
Heb. 10:19-22

Does reading these verses change your answer in any way? How? Let's see if we can spell it out for you without getting too deep in Christian theology.

In the beginning humans sinned against God. Despite the fact that God was greatly saddened, He chose to love us anyway.

God cannot stand the presence of sin. Since humans became sinful creatures, God provided a means to have our sins cleansed via a sacrificial offering. If humans sacrificed a perfect animal, God would forgive their sins. It was the shedding of that perfect animal's blood that did the trick.

Unfortunately for us, that was only a temporary fix. God knew that too. He allowed humans to struggle under the weight of a system of laws. These laws were set up so we could live in harmony with God. But as hard as humans tried, we just couldn't do it on our own.

Because God wanted an intimate relationship with us, He became like us. God sent himself to earth in the form of His Son, Jesus. Jesus was God in the flesh. His life painted a picture of God's love and forgiveness toward us. Jesus became the ultimate perfect sacrifice for us. He shed His blood for us so we wouldn't have to live under the old rules anymore. If you miss anything else, don't miss this:

- God required a bloody sacrifice for the forgiveness of sins.

- God knew we would never be able to find ultimate fulfillment on our own.

- God willingly became the ultimate bloody sacrifice once and for all because of His amazing love for us!

That's right. God died for us to show us He was willing to do whatever it takes to draw us back to Him.

Well, I feel like I've really messed up. And worse yet, I'm afraid I'll keep messing up. Will God eventually get tired of that and just give up on me?

Many people believe God is sitting in heaven waiting to drop-kick us out of His kingdom as soon as we mess up. And while it's true that God hates sin, God does not want you to fail. In fact, nothing could be farther from the truth! If God really wanted to blast us to kingdom come every time we sin, He'd never have sent Jesus in the first place. Do you think God would have gone through the trouble and pain if that was His agenda? But when we do cross the line, it's important to realize it and to rectify the situation. This is what the Bible has to say about that:

    1 John 1:5—2:2

    Rom. 10:9-13

    2 Cor. 5:21

God wants to forgive you. He doesn't get tired of doing it. That's why Jesus died in the first place.

So if Jesus did all this for me, how do I begin living the way He wants me to?

Once again, the answers are found in the Word. Read each of the following scriptures; then compose a paragraph in the space provided, giving a synopsis of what you've read.

Rom. 6:10-13

1 Pet. 2:17-18

1 Pet. 2:1-5

Titus 3:1-6

Living a Christ-centered life is God's goal for us. That means we attempt to do everything as Jesus would have done. God realizes we aren't perfect, but His desire is for us to experience the joy of a Christ-centered life. Wrap up this session by reading 1 Tim. 4:7-12. That should be our goal in life. This week we'll dig deeper into that concept and show you how to do it.

Day 8: Religion vs. Christianity

Life from Death

For the wages of sin is death, but the gift of God is eternal life in Christ Jesus our Lord (Rom. 6:23).

Adrenaline coursed through Jeff's veins as he climbed into the backseat of Brian's '69 Mustang. He secured himself with the seatbelt as his best friend, Robert, slid into the front passenger seat, slamming the door behind him. The interior of the car felt like an oven, and Robert rolled down the window.

"You've never cruised with Brian before, have you?" Robert asked. Jeff's eyes were wide with excitement as he shook his head. "Then get ready for the ride of your life!"

Jeff grinned and cinched the seatbelt a little tighter. Brian was known as the school's fastest driver, and he'd never been pulled over by the police. There were rumors that Brian had some sort of magic about him, that he never could be stopped. Some had gone so far as to say he'd even broken the sound barrier with his car. Brian was a legend.

Brian's quirky personality added to his status. Very few teens really knew him well, although most wanted to. Always dressed in black, he was a young man of few words. Yet he was always the center of conversation. Jeff considered himself lucky just to sit in Brian's Mustang—much less cruise with him.

Brian crawled behind the wheel. He rolled down his window to vent the summer heat. He glanced into the rearview mirror at Jeff and nodded. Then, like an ancient predator coming back from the grave, Brian's machine rumbled to life. Jeff began to wonder if the rumors that Brian had secretly installed a jet engine under the hood were actually true. Suddenly the Mustang squealed out of the parking lot and zoomed down a remote country road.

"Here's where it gets fun," Robert said.

Jeff gasped as the car screamed toward a dead animal lying in the middle of the road. Jeff remembered a rumor about Brian's nasty habit of dive-bombing roadkill.

Suddenly—thump! Pink and black guts splattered the road. Brian and Robert whooped in the front seat. Jeff couldn't quite believe what had just happened. Yet as disgusting a habit as it was, Jeff found himself strangely fascinated by the whole episode. As the guys in the front seat cackled laughter, Jeff found himself chuckling along. Despite the sickening nature of Brian's roadkill dive-bombing, Jeff secretly hoped they would come across another dead animal soon so he could witness it one more time.

Think About It!

Most of us have seen a scary movie or two. There's something about when the music starts to build and the tension is riding high that hooks us. We don't want to watch what's going to happen, and yet we can't turn our eyes away from the screen. We just have to see what's going to happen. Humans have this weird attraction to the shocking.

In the same way, humanity also has a sad attraction to sin as well. We try all we can on our own, but still, sin has us and on our own we just can't keep away from it. Just like Jeff was strangely drawn to another dive-bomb run, humans are drawn to sin even if we know it's the worst thing for us.

Humans are sinful creatures. We don't like to face that fact because it's not a very nice thought. We can deny it all we want, but it doesn't change the cold truth of it. And left to our own, we would completely destroy ourselves.

For some reason, God loved us so much He wanted to rescue us from that fate. Who really knows why? Only God really knows the reason He wanted to provide salvation to humanity. We rejected Him in the beginning. We still do to this day. And yet knowing that His love for us would still be scorned, He gave it anyway. Wow!

God loved us so much that He became one of His own creatures. He became flesh and blood through the person of Jesus so He could feel and be just like us. He left His celestial throne and was born a human.

He grew up a human. He was a child and then a teenager just like us. He had chores and worked in His father's shop. His hands were callused from pounding a hammer all day long. His muscles were strong from sawing wood and lifting lumber. He was a man just like any other.

When He reached His 30s, He left His job, gathered 12 unlikely companions, and began showing the world what God was really like. People's lives were changed forever when they met Jesus. He healed, fed, taught, walked with, laughed with, cried with, blessed, and moved them. And yet humanity still rejected Him. But that's what God expected. Finally humanity nailed Jesus to a cross, thinking that would be the end of the story. But that was only the beginning!

Three days later, Jesus was raised from the dead and walked out of the grave. God's incredible power conquered death for us! As a result, Jesus offers us life. He offers to take away our lust for sin and replace it with a passion for life and a dream for a spectacular future. And we choose whether to accept death at our own hands or life in His.

Salvation! We can't understand it or figure it out. We shouldn't try to because we never will. Just accept it and believe it.

Explore these scriptures:

Feed Your Face

Eph. 2:1-10

1 John 4:7-15

John 5:19-27

Check the truth. Get a good Bible concordance and find several good references to the words "saved" and "salvation." Dig in and see what else the Bible has to say about this subject.

Deal with it. Ask God to give you a clearer idea of what salvation really means. So often we take it for granted. We don't have a clear picture of Jesus' sacrifice. God will give you a deeper appreciation for His gift.

Day 9: Religion vs. Relationship

Oh—Another Day!

Therefore, if anyone is in Christ, he is a new creation; the old has gone, the new has come! (2 Cor. 5:17).

Let's drop in on Cheryl:

It was 6 A.M., and the alarm clock screamed early-morning aggravation. Still half sleeping, Cheryl found and pressed the snooze button.

She dozed another restless five minutes. The alarm blared again. Another automatic reaction turned it off for good, and she crawled out of bed.

Cheryl stumbled to the bathroom, her mouth gaping in yawns along the way. The light above the small vanity blazed like a thousand suns. Tired fingers rubbed crusties from her eyes. Another miserable morning, she thought.

She frowned at herself in the mirror. Her bushy hair was everywhere and wild, like a dust mop. Her face was red-lined from where it had been on her wrinkled pillow throughout the night.

Mechanically she got ready for school. She didn't have to think about it. Same as every other day: shower, fix hair, do makeup, get dressed, eat Frosted Flakes, brush teeth, check makeup once again. Nothing ever changed. But why should it? This was her life every morning. Habit. Monotony. A rut. Boring!

Several minutes later she was headed down toward the kitchen, dodging her three-year-old brat of a brother on the way. She plopped her backpack down on the kitchen counter, grabbed her lunch from the fridge, and threw it in on top of her books.

"Sleep well?" her mom asked.

"Like a queen," Cheryl sarcastically snapped back. *Like she cares*, Cheryl thought to herself.

"Have a good day at school, honey," called her dad as she headed toward the front door. Cheryl threw a well-practiced fake smile over her shoulder toward her parents and slammed the front door behind her.

Let's drop in on Todd:

It was 6 A.M., and the alarm clock screamed early-morning aggravation. Todd reached for the snooze button but couldn't find it. He stretched blindly with his hand. Unfortunately, his efforts only succeeded in knocking it off the nightstand. As if in retaliation, the clock amplified itself three decibel levels.

Wide awake now, Todd reached for the fallen source of morning paranoia, which was inches from his extended fingertips. He stretched, lost his balance, and tumbled out of bed in a heap.

Lying on the floor, he yanked the clock cord out of the wall. Silence—finally. He closed his eyes again.

How easy it would be, Todd thought, *to just lie here all day. It's not like anyone would know . . . or care*. Ever since his mom died four months ago, there were often mornings such as today. He often wondered why the early morning hours were so brutal on a person's memories.

Even now, if he thought hard enough, he could still remember the smell of bacon and eggs, the aroma of his dad's coffee. Breakfast together had been a morning ritual for his family. *Now, with Mom gone and with Dad having to work a second job, we're lucky to even see each other for more than an hour or so a day*, he reminded himself. The task of preparing breakfast for himself and his younger brother, Tony, had fallen to Todd.

Lifting himself off the floor, Todd walked down the hall and peeked into his brother's room. *Still asleep*. Todd smiled, deciding not to wake Tony just yet. He'd take a quick shower, get dressed, then wake his brother.

Twenty minutes later, Todd was downstairs, popping open a can of biscuits and arranging them on a baking sheet. *Not quite the same as Mom's homemade breakfasts*, Todd admitted, but he was getting better at it.

Tony would be downstairs soon. In a funny sort of way, Todd and his brother had grown closer than ever during the past couple of months.

Todd didn't know quite how to explain it, but things were getting better. Life sure wasn't "normal"—whatever that meant—but things were improving.

As he and Tony sat down for a quick breakfast, Todd prayed, *Thanks, God, for another day. I'm not sure what's ahead for us; but, with Your help, I know we're gonna make it!*

Think About It! **Two people, both facing a new day but approaching it completely different.** One gets ready for the day out of obligation. *If I have to I'll do it, but I won't like it* is Cheryl's mind-set. No thrill for what the day holds. No excitement. Just get it done. Todd, on the other hand, approaches the day with anticipation. From the moment he gets out of bed, life is an adventure. Sure sometimes it's rough, but it's another day that God has given us. Another day to live, to grow, to heal, to laugh, to become. In spite of our circumstances, we must realize the enormous potential each new day holds in store.

In a sense those scenarios are a lot like the way we approach God. Either we approach Him because we have to, out of obligation, not expecting much; or we come to Him wanting an incredible journey, excited about the prospects and anxious to experience God.

God desires a relationship with us. Relationships are vibrant. They are constantly changing and growing. Through a relationship with Him we grow much more.

He doesn't want our "religion." Religion by itself is doing something out of burden, not out of desire. There's no life in simple religion. It's dull and can seem more like a chore. God wants intimacy with us. He wants our relationship with Him to be full of excitement and anticipation of the great things ahead in our walk with Him.

So how do we have a relationship and not just religion? It starts by how we approach God. Realize that God isn't a taskmaster waiting to crush us as soon as we mess up. He's loving, caring, patient, and wants the best for us. He wants to be our ultimate Friend—one who will do anything to get close to us. If that's the case (and it is!), spending time with God gets easier and more exciting each day.

Explore these scriptures:

Feed Your Face

Rom. 8:1-17

1 Pet. 1:3-8

Col. 2:6-12

Get it right. Think about the fact that God loves you beyond anything. Nothing you could ever do will separate you from that love (Rom. 8:38-39). God wants to become best friends with you.

Formulas don't exist. When you spend time with God, there's no specific way you have to do it. There aren't any particular words you have to say. There aren't special passages you have to read. It's just you and Him. Talk and share with Him as you would with any other person you might know.

Day 10: Prayer

Where Were You?

Then Jesus told his disciples a parable to show them that they should always pray and not give up (Luke 18:1).

"Jennifer!"

Jennifer turned to see Kayla swerving through the crowded hall toward her. Jennifer placed her remaining books in the locker, slammed it shut, and walked away. She didn't want to deal with Kayla.

"Where are you going?" Kayla asked, grabbing Jennifer's arm.

"I've got class, Kayla," Jennifer snapped.

"But I need to talk to you. It's important! I need your help with something."

"Well, it'll have to wait, Kayla. I have to go." Jennifer sternly turned to walk away again.

"Some friend you are! Here I am in need, and you walk away. What's your problem?"

Jennifer froze. An icy chill ran down her back. Immediately a tense pounding began in her head as her blood pressure skyrocketed. Digging her nails into her palms, she calmed herself. How dare Kayla accuse her of being a bad friend?

"Excuse me?" she hissed as she wheeled around. "Are you accusing me of not being a good friend?"

"You don't see me walking away, do you?"

Jennifer swallowed hard and ground her teeth. "I've called you every day for the last week, and you haven't returned even one of my calls."

"Did you ever stop to think that maybe I didn't get the messages?"

"I asked your mother last night. She said she's given you every message."

"Oh," Kayla fumbled, "I've been pretty busy studying for finals."

"Busy?" Jennifer was livid.

"You don't have to raise your voice at me."

"Kayla, my grandmother passed away last week! You knew it too! I needed a friend, and you snubbed me! How dare you accuse me of poor friendship?"

"Jennifer, calm down," Kayla insisted. A crowd was gathering, and she didn't like to make a scene. "I know your grandmother died and all. I'm sorry I didn't return your calls. It's just that—well—Damon broke up with me, and I didn't think I could take anything else."

Jennifer tasted blood. It took a second for her to realize she was biting her lip. Her heart was pounding. Before her stood the girl she thought was her best friend. She didn't want a scene either. She hadn't been prepared for this moment. She took several deep, soothing breaths. "I can't talk to you right now, Kayla. I've got to go to class." With that, Jennifer spun on her heels and burst through the doors behind her.

"But, Jennifer, I said I'm sorry," Kayla called. "Call me tonight. OK?"

Think About It! **Communication is the key to keeping any relationship alive.** Without communication there can be no relationship. There is a direct correlation between the amount of communication and the strength of the relationship. In other words, the more we talk with someone, the better friends we are with him or her. If communication dwindles, so does the relationship.

Here's another fact: There are no one-way relationships. Person A can't be best friends with Person B if Person B doesn't give a rip about the relationship. It just doesn't happen.

It's the same way in our relationship with God. If we're going to get to know Him, we have to communicate with Him. We communicate with God through prayer. The more we pray, the closer friends we are with Him. No prayer = no friendship. Jesus spent time in prayer. If He put such importance on prayer and He was God's Son, we should take a clue from His example.

There are lots of people out there who have formulas on proper prayer techniques. There are even those who say proper prayer can happen only at certain times of the day. But the truth is that prayer is based on a personal relationship with God. There are no correct words.

There are no established formats. It's simple discussion between us and God. We can say whatever we like—we aren't going to shock God. He heard worse, believe me. He can bear it. And we can pray whenever we like—morning, evening, in study hall, before bedtime. We have to choose what time works best for us.

The only hard-and-fast rule is this: If we're going to grow in our relationship with God, we have to pray on a daily basis. Remember: if there's no communication, there's no relationship.

Explore these scriptures:

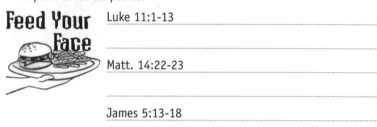

Feed Your Face

Luke 11:1-13

Matt. 14:22-23

James 5:13-18

Evaluate your schedule. Examine everything you do on a daily basis. Find the best time for you to spend with God in prayer. Is it mornings before the day begins, afternoons when school lets out, evenings before you go to bed? Try to find a time you can consistently meet with God and share with Him.

Open your ears. After you've spent time sharing what you're dealing with, spend time listening to God. That means doing nothing. Listen to what your heart tells you. Tune into your conscience. Give God time to speak to you.

Day 11: The Word
What Directions?

I have hidden your word in my heart that I might not sin against you (Ps. 119:11).

Beth pulled the oven mitt over her hand. With a deep, anxious breath she slowly pried the oven door open and peered inside. A cloud of black smoke billowed out and into her face. Coughing and gagging, she let the door slam shut with a resounding crash. Frantically she rubbed her burning, tearing eyes with the oven mitt as she heaved for fresh air. Unfortunately, each gasp drew in more of the charred stench. Gagging, she stumbled to the kitchen door, resting against the door frame for support.

Ruined! An hour's worth of work wasted.

Moments later the stinging in her eyes stopped and she regained her breath. She opened a window for ventilation and turned on the fan above the oven. Then, she flung open the oven door and leaped backward several feet. Once again an ashen cloud mushroomed from inside.

In one swift movement Beth thrust her mitted hand inside, extracted the smoldering cake pan, and kicked the oven door shut. Then she tossed the smoking pan onto the counter.

Tears once again welled up in her eyes—this time not because of smoke. She slammed the oven mitt down.

"What's burning?" her mother asked, sticking her head into the kitchen. She noticed the blackened dish on the counter. "Oh, your cake!"

Beth nodded silently and rubbed a tear from her cheek. Her mother came to her side, encasing her in a loving arm.

"It was supposed to be for Ron," Beth sniffed. Ron was her boy-friend. "His birthday's today, and I wanted to make something special for him. Now it's ruined."

"That's OK, honey," her mother soothed, "you can try again."

Beth shook her head. "No, I don't have time. I have to get cleaned up and go to his house. I'm supposed to be there in 30 minutes." She crossed her arms in frustration.

"What went wrong?" her mother asked.

"I don't know. I thought I did everything like you always do it."

"Well, you followed the recipe, didn't you?"

"As best I could remember," Beth choked.

Her mother pursed her lips trying not to laugh. "Beth, I've been cooking for years. I know a lot about cooking, but I still always follow the recipe. It's too easy to get the directions mixed up if you don't." Beth nodded in silence. Her mother ran her fingers through Beth's hair. "Go get ready, and I'll clean this up for you. Then we'll run by the gro-cery store and pick up a cake on the way to Ron's house."

Beth plodded toward the door. Before she stepped out, she looked back. "Thanks, Mom," she said.

Her mother smiled. "You're welcome."

Beth disappeared down the hall.

"What a mess!" her mom said, smiling as she tossed the charred cake remains into the trash.

Think About It! **Knowing the truth and figuring out God's will aren't the easiest things in the world to do.** In fact, those two aspects of Christianity can be pretty nebulous. Fortunately for us, God gave us directions. Those directions are contained in the Bible. More than just a book of cool stories, poetic verses, and uplifting promises, the Bible is actually God's Word. He spoke to men of ages past, and they wrote down every word His Spirit inspired them to.

There's kind of a supernatural thing to God's Word. I mean, accord-ing to Genesis, God spoke the world into existence. And Jesus fought off Satan in the wilderness not with His fists or a cocky attitude—but with God's Word. The spoken Word of God has power, and we've been given authority to use it.

The other neat point is that God speaks to us through His Word. When we read His Word, He tells us very clearly what He wants us to know. So if we want to get a grip on what God's got planned for us, we need to get into the Word. If we want to find out what makes God tick, we need to get into the Word. If we want to hear the voice of God and apply it to our lives, we need to get into the Word.

Every time we meet with God, we should spend some of that time in the Bible. The best part is that the more we spend time with Him and in the Word, the more we become like God! It's almost like God's Word takes root in us and starts growing. The Word becomes a part of us! It's unexplainable. It's indescribable. But it's a fact, and it's awesome!

Explore these scriptures:

Feed Your Face

2 Tim. 3:14-17

Ps. 119:12-24

James 1:19-25

Get with the plan. Plan to read the Bible, but don't just begin reading at Genesis and head to the end. You'll probably bog down around Leviticus or Numbers and never make it through. Ask your pastor, youth pastor, or youth leader if he or she has a Bible reading plan. Most plans take you on an interesting and orderly journey that keeps you from losing interest. Get a copy, and start digging into God's Word.

Start here if nowhere else. If you can't find a reading plan right away, start by reading the books of John and Romans. Try reading about a chapter a day at first. If it's really good and you want more, feel free to increase the size of passages you take in at your leisure. But continue to search for a good reading plan while you devour John and Romans.

Commit it to memory. Along with reading the Bible, begin the process of memorizing verses that really speak to you. The more of God's Word you have in your head, the closer you'll grow to Him.

Day 12: Spiritual Responsibility
What Red Light?

Do not let this Book of the Law depart from your mouth; meditate on it day and night, so that you may be careful to do everything written in it. Then you will be prosperous and successful (Josh. 1:8).

Kevin jumped in his car and slammed the door. He was running late for school. He jammed the key into the ignition and twisted it abruptly. The engine grumbled its annoyance. He looked at his watch. He'd never make it on time. The engine turned over three more times and roared to life. It seemed to be rattling a little more than usual this morning.

It's just because of the cold weather, thought Kevin.

He yanked the gear shift into reverse and screeched out of the driveway, narrowly missing the mailbox. Slamming the gear into drive, he stomped on the pedal and thundered down the street as white smoke poured out of the tailpipe. He noticed it in the rearview mirror.

It must be colder out than I'd noticed.

He checked the speedometer to make sure he wasn't going too fast. He was cruising at 45 mph. The speed limit was 40. That would have to do. He couldn't afford another ticket. A red light next to the speedometer beamed at him. The oil light. It had first blinked on a week ago. He'd been forgetting to put oil in every day since. Last night his dad had warned him to take care of it or he'd be sorry. Kevin promised himself he'd take care of it as soon as school was over.

I can't afford to stop now. If I am late again I'll get detention for sure!

Kevin jabbed the power button on his new stereo. It took several seconds for the amplifiers to warm up. When they did, the entire car vibrated to the bone-jarring music. Kevin drummed the steering wheel with both hands and sang along.

His stereo seemed to be pumping more amperage than usual today. The old heap shook a little more than normal. Kevin nodded a silent approval and grinned in pride.

In the rearview mirror he noticed the car was still pumping out the smoke. He checked the temperature gauge. It showed the car was hot, too hot. Then he noticed the speedometer was dropping rapidly. He stomped the pedal. Nothing happened. He turned the radio down. No engine noise. Reaching for the keys, he turned them over but nothing happened. He did it again. As the car slowed to a halt, a wave of nausea swept through Kevin. He knew what had happened: the engine had locked up due to lack of oil.

"No! Why God? Why?" he shouted.

Think About It! **Routine maintenance:** lots of things require it—cars, toilets, computers, backyard gardens, our teeth, our bodies, our spiritual lives. That's right; our spiritual lives need regular maintenance as well. Only our spiritual lives can't afford to be put off the way other things can. We have a responsibility to recharge our batteries daily.

Most of us have heard the same old story: someone accepts Christ as their Savior and then within a week it's back to business as usual—as if nothing had ever happened. They thought all they'd have to do is accept Christ and that was it. Jesus would come in, cleanse them, and magically change their life completely.

Well, that can and does happen with many people. The difference is that people who grow in the Lord begin maintaining the gift God gave them from the very beginning. Those who don't grow in the Lord are the selfish and lazy ones. They want the gift of life but don't want to give anything in return. It really doesn't take much to pick up God's Word and spend a few minutes each day with Him. Instead, they'd rather go back to the miserable way they were. Then they blame God as if it's His fault that they didn't get all He had in store for them.

The truth is that God has all the joy, love, hope, and peace we need just waiting on us in order to face life. But He can't give it to us if we won't spend time listening and talking with Him. Turning our lives around is God's responsibility. He completes His end of the bargain when we spend time with Him. Making time for God is our responsibility.

Explore these scriptures:

Feed Your Face

2 Pet. 1:2-11

Eph. 4:17-24

Luke 9:23-26

Analyze the past. Since you've become a Christian, how often have you gone through spiritual struggles or dry spots? When you went through them, were you staying in the Word? Did your time with God suffer? Often it's a lack of devotion that causes people to languish spiritually. Next time you feel dead inwardly, get back in God's Word.

Day 13: Humble Service
Feeling Dirty

And being found in appearance as a man, [Jesus] humbled himself and became obedient to death—even death on a cross! (Phil. 2:8).

"I don't want to hang around all those dirty, scummy people!" Cheryl complained, hearing she was going to a homeless shelter to help out. The last thing she wanted to do was deal with people who couldn't get their lives together.

"Sorry you feel that way," her youth pastor stated briskly, clearly perturbed at her arrogant attitude. "That's your as-signment. Either you work at the homeless shelter, or you can get someone else to monitor your community service hours."

Cheryl was applying to a private college. Part of her being accepted required that she perform 40 hours of community service. Those hours had to be overseen by her pastor, youth pastor, or a teacher.

A homeless shelter? Cheryl reluctantly agreed. The application dead-line was next week, and she didn't have time to set up anything with one of her teachers.

I don't want to hang around all those dirty, scummy people!

She arrived early in the morning. When she walked through the door, she immediately felt out of place. But the manager of the shelter was very kind. She sat Cheryl behind a desk doing office work for the vast majority of the day. It wasn't that bad after all.

But when it came time for the evening meal, the shelter was short on people in the serving line. They slapped a plastic apron on Cheryl and stuck her hairspray-plastered curls into a hair net. Then they handed her a serving spoon and stuck her behind the counter.

I don't want to hang around all those dirty, scummy people!

People filed by, slowly holding their trays out toward her. Some smiled and some didn't. Some looked stoned on cheap wine and crack. Others looked as if they could have lived right next door to Cheryl.

A family came through with two small girls. They were polite and thanked Cheryl for the food she placed on their trays. The girls were both young, not even in grade school yet. Their parents looked healthy. *How could they be homeless?* Both the girls were dressed in dingy hand-me-downs. Cheryl wondered if they'd even had a bath in the last week. So young. So innocent.

She was silent as she drove home. Deep in thought, she didn't bother turning on the radio. *I don't want to hang around all those dirty, scummy people!* The statement replayed in her mind like a broken record. As she halted at a stop light, she glanced down at her jeans. They had picked up grease stains from the serving line. She grimaced, knowing they wouldn't come clean. Cheryl thought of the two little girls. For the price of these jeans she could have paid for two small outfits for them alone.

I don't want to hang around all those dirty, scummy people!

Suddenly Cheryl felt dirty all over.

Think About It! **From His birth to His death on a cross,** Jesus' life is a shining example of humility and service. He gave up His heavenly throne only to be born in a stable. His first bed was a feeding trough. He grew up a working man, a carpenter. He fed thousands who were hungry.

He touched and healed those with sores and wounds oozing with pus when the doctors wouldn't even come near them. He reached out to those who no one else wanted around. He brought laughter and joy to the brokenhearted. Those whom society rejected, He gathered around Him as His friends. He washed the grimy feet of those same friends and in the end allowed himself to be nailed to a shameful cross—the death sentence reserved for the worst of criminals.

He lived His life on earth as the human representative of God. That's right. From cover to cover, the Bible challenges us to live a life of humility, of service to others. Putting others before ourselves is the anthem that rings throughout.

Often enough, the only rewards for humility are inner joy and favor with God—not a bad return for the investment. Of course, we can't put those rewards on a trophy shelf and show them off to everyone. But if we wanted to do that, we'd probably never win the award for humility to start off with.

Explore these scriptures:

Feed Your Face

Rom. 12:4-13

Acts 6:1-6

John 13:3-15

Go out and drive. Get your youth group or your school friends together and organize a citywide food drive. Collect canned and nonperishable foods and donate them to a local food bank. Or if you prefer, make up food baskets of your own and give them to those in your church or community who are needy.

Check your heart. If the truth be known, most of us do not have very humble hearts. Society and the media drive us to be self-centered individuals. Spend time in prayer, asking God to show you areas in your life in which you need to work on humility and service. Then commit to putting humble service into action.

Day 14: Sacrifice

Giving It Up

*Therefore, I urge you, brothers, in view of God's mercy, to offer
your bodies as living sacrifices, holy and pleasing to God—this
is your spiritual act of worship (Rom. 12:1).*

Jennifer lay restlessly on her bed, her right arm stretched out, inches from her phone. Her eyes lingered again on a gold-framed picture of Brandon, her boyfriend.

She hated decisions like this. She looked down once more at the tickets she held in her left hand. Box seats, she thought. She and Brandon had talked for months about wanting to see the latest Andrew Lloyd Webber musical. Now they had been given two tickets! They had been thrilled, at least until they looked at the date of the show.

For four years Brandon had practiced, played, endured, improved, and conquered high school baseball. His team had won the last three years' state championships, led there by his pitching. He had also made the regional all-star team for the last two years.

With his senior year winding down, Brandon was getting nervous. He had been hoping for an athletic scholarship to State Tech. His grades and athletic ability were certainly good enough. Yet no scholarship had materialized. He had received offers from other colleges but none from his dream school.

His coach had informed him that Tech was looking at him. Scouts from Tech had attended their games. But there was a pitcher in the neighboring state they were also considering. Tech's scout planned on being at this year's all-star game for one more look at Brandon's pitching before they made their decision.

That's where Jennifer's dilemma began. The musical was the evening of the all-star game. With the game being played in Oak Grove—a five-hour drive—there was no chance they'd be able to make both commitments.

There had been one awkward moment when they first realized the conflict. "Under normal circumstances this would have been a no-brainer. I'd ditch the game. It's just a game to honor us 'hot-shots'!" Brandon had explained, smiling. "But this year's game is different. It could drastically affect my life for the next few years."

Looking back, Jennifer knew that Brandon's hesitation was mainly due to his desire not to disappoint her. *That's Brandon,* she smiled, *sensitive as ever!*

She assured him that everything was OK with her, that she understood why he had to be at the game. She'd be able to find someone else to go to the show with her. "It's not a big deal," Jennifer had said. "Don't worry about it."

Yet, now, Jennifer was worried. She'd been feeling increasingly concerned about not being there to support Brandon. Brandon was the best thing that had ever happened to her. Because of him, Jennifer had become a Christian. They had been dating for the last two and a half years. She loved him. She eventually wanted to marry him.

He's pitched games without me before. He'll do fine. And yet something was making Jennifer question her priorities. *After all, it is just a musical. And the tickets were free—it's not like we'll be out a lot of money.*

Jennifer spent a few more minutes arguing with herself in her mind and then picked up the phone and called her best friend. "Hey, Keri," she began. "You know that new show we've all wanted to see? How would you and Ben like two free tickets?"

Think About It!

Giving up something you want for the good of something or someone else. That's not a very technical definition of what sacrifice means, but it will do. And that's exactly what God calls us to do. But why?

There are lots of reasons for sacrifice. But the best reason is because when we sacrifice, God receives more glory, and we grow spiritually.

How's that?

We live in a society that is completely self-centered. The world challenges us to do everything for ourselves because "we deserve it." That flies in the face of what Jesus told us to do. He said put God first, others next in line, and then consider ourselves. That's the key to true happiness. There's an inner joy we receive when we put God and others first.

Does that mean I have to give up everything?

Not necessarily. But it does mean we have to be willing if God asks us to. And it's true that sometimes it's not easy at all to sacrifice. It sounds crazy and a bit frightening. But God never asks anything from us that He doesn't return in abundance in some way. And the reward for obedience is far greater than the price of disobedience. And don't forget that Jesus made the ultimate sacrifice for us already—*He gave His own life!*

So what do I sacrifice?

Don't worry. If you're spending time with Him, He'll let you know. And when you do know, don't hesitate. Just give it up and see what happens.

Explore these scriptures:

Feed Your Face

Matt. 6:19-24

2 Cor. 8:1-9

2 Cor. 9:6-11

Go to the Source. Ask God to give you a generous heart. Ask Him to provide ways for you to give sacrificially. Then trust Him to provide ways.

Don't miss your chance. When you see ways that you can put others first, jump at the opportunity even if it's just a little thing like holding the door open for someone. Generosity and kindness are the evidence of a sacrificial heart.

Give it some thought. Look at everything you spend your time and money on. Find something you really like but could do without. Make a sacrifice. If it's something you spend money on, give the money in turn to God. If it's a time issue, spend that time with God.

SECTION 3
RIGHTEOUS RELATIONSHIPS

Wake-Up Call
Weekly Bible Study

Made to Be Social

Consider some of the world's most famous relationships: Antony and Cleopatra, Mary and Joseph, Brad and Angelina. Chances are each began with a first glance, and then led to a first conversation. Before long, strangers turned into acquaintances—then into casual, close, or intimate friends.

So how's your social life? Do you want more friends? (Stupid question, right—because we all do.) Does the possibility of dating have your stomach tied into a bunch of knots? Do you feel like a social outcast and fear that you'll end up spending your whole life alone? Is your friendship with Jesus suffering?

Regardless of where you are on the friendship scale, let's spend this week exploring our social nature—from friendship to dating to marriage to knowing God more intimately. And in the process, let's seek to discover how we can improve—and ultimately be transformed into the kind of "Christian friend" God wants us to be.

● Think of a moment when you felt like an outsider—maybe even an alien. How did a friend help you? Why are friends important to you?

● Recall a time when a friend hurt you.

How did you react?
What are some steps that you can take to improve communication with your friend?
What should you do when a friend gets mad at you?
Why are put-downs so destructive?

● Think about all your friends at school or in your youth group. Which category below do they fit in (and why)?

CASUAL   CLOSE   INTIMATE

● Crack open your Bible and read 1 Cor. 13:1-13. Pick five qualities of love from this passage and apply them to a friendship you're in right now.

   Based on this passage, how does God want us to treat each other?
   How does your friend measure up?
   Is he or she building you up and drawing you closer to God?
   Is your friend pulling you away from God?

● For the next couple of minutes, let's look to the future. Think about your idea of an ideal marriage partner.

Give lots of details: List appearance, career choices, personality, intelligence, and spiritual convictions.

   How do current and past dating partners fit your description above?

● What does the Bible have to say about sex? Check out the following passages; then share what you think God wants us to understand about sex.

Gen. 1:26-28

1 Tim. 4:4-5

Gen. 38:9

Deut. 24:5

Prov. 5:18-20

Section 3: RIGHTEOUS RELATIONSHIPS

1 Cor. 6:18-20

1 Cor. 7:3-4

● Why do you think it's important for married couples to express their love in a physical way?

● Name three significant ways in which love is different from lust (for help, check out 1 Cor. 13:1-13).

● How far is too far for teenagers who date? Based on what you've read in the Scriptures, as well as what you've experienced in a past or current dating relationship, check off the physical actions that you believe are wrong.

- ❏ holding hands ❏ lying together ❏ prolonged kissing
- ❏ being alone together for an extended period of time
- ❏ touching each other's "private areas" ❏ hugging
- ❏ back rubs ❏ light kissing ❏ close dancing

● Explain why you checked off the activities above.

_____

_____

_____

_____

● Why is sexual purity the best choice?

_____

_____

_____

_____

Day 15: Peer Groups

So Many Choices

For many are invited, but few are chosen (Matt. 22:14).

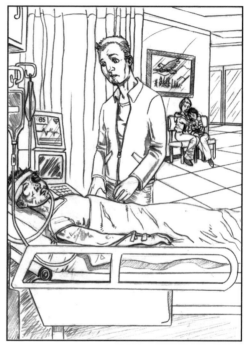

The phone rang, jarring Rich from a deep slumber. He rolled over, propped himself on an elbow, and looked at the clock—2:30 A.M. He collapsed back into the comfort of his bed and tried to ignore it.

Who could be calling at this hour? Maybe they'll hang up. But they didn't. The phone kept ringing.

"Are you going to get that?" moaned his wife, Gloria, next to him in the bed. She pulled the blanket up over her head as if that would protect her from the phone's nocturnal onslaught. Rich's fingers found the receiver and picked it up.

"Hello," he growled, annoyed at being awakened at this hour. There was a long silence as the person on the other end apologized for waking him and then explained the reason for call.

"Oh, no," Rich whispered breaking the quietness of the night. He sat up and swung his feet to the floor. "I'll be there." He hung up.

"What's wrong?" Gloria asked, sensing the urgency.

"It's Brian. He's been in a serious car accident. They say he might not make it." Rich flipped the night-light on.

Gloria drew in her breath. Her mind raced through all conceivable possibilities that could have caused such a disaster. Rich read the troubled look on her face.

"He was out partying," he stated, answering her unasked question.

Within five minutes of the phone call Rich was headed for the hospital. No doubt there would be other teens from his youth group there. This kind of news had a way of traveling fast, even at 3 A.M. He rehearsed lines of encouragement to offer if needed but knew the effort was pointless. He wouldn't remember them in the end.

As he walked through the emergency room doors, his suspicions were confirmed. Two young ladies almost knocked him over when they saw him. They clung to Rich like rag dolls, weeping uncontrollably, needing support from their youth pastor. He wrapped his arms around them and calmed them down. Then depositing them in the two nearest chairs, he stepped to the reception desk. After he explained who he was, a nurse ushered him to Brian's cubicle.

Brian lay there unconscious, almost unrecognizable. His long brown hair was half shaved off where they'd sewn his skull back together. The wreck had thrown him through the windshield. What hair was left was matted in blood, and his face was bruised purple. A tube snaked down his throat so he could breathe, and his arm was pinned with several intravenous tubes. The rest of his body told a similar story—cut, stitched, and bruised.

Rich grimaced.

Three years ago Brian was a bright, energetic eighth grader. He was always being called down for rowdiness, but what eighth grader wasn't? Since then Rich had noticed Brian hanging out with a rougher crowd. Despite Rich's efforts to the contrary, he'd seen Brian slipping away from God. Recently he had even refused to attend church at all, saying he didn't need it. Rich urged him on several occasions to look at where his life was headed. Brian had laughed at him. Rich warned Brian that his new friends were dragging him down. Brian had laughed again.

Rich shook his head and placed his hand on Brian's arm.

"Why, Brian?"

 **Think About It!** **We make a lot of choices in our lives.** We choose what our favorite food or our favorite radio station is. We choose what clothes we'll wear, when we get up in the morning, or whether to brush our teeth before we go to bed at night. Some choices

are important. Some don't really matter. Some won't shape our lives. Others will.

One of the most important choices we make that shapes our lives is who our friends are. We don't get to choose our family members. Win, lose, or draw, we're stuck with them. But we can choose our peers.

Studies have shown that who we choose to hang out with has a large effect on our life decisions. If that's the case, we need to choose our friends wisely. To think nothing of whom we associate with is foolishness. Regardless of whether we want to believe it or not, our peer groups can shape where we are tomorrow. Peer groups can vault us to new heights or drag us to unwanted lows. It's our choice.

Jesus chose His friends carefully. He gathered a group of guys around Him who had potential to change the world. That's exactly what they did too. Will we do the same? Will we hang with world-changers, or will our peer groups cause us to be dramatically less than God intended?

Explore these scriptures:

Feed Your Face

Luke 6:12-16

Prov. 27:6-10

Acts 9:17-29

Go to the Source. God is the closest Friend we can have. Ask Him to help you develop righteous friendships that will build you up instead of drag you down.

Take inventory. Make a list of all the people you call your friends. Beside each name, honestly evaluate whether that person is a good or bad influence on you. If he or she is a good influence, plan ways in which you can get to know that individual better. If he or she is a bad influence (and this will be the tough one), consider whether you really want to keep that person as a close friend. It doesn't mean you're going to abandon him or her all together. It simply means you won't deepen that relationship to the point where it becomes a destructive force in your life. And you don't have to say anything to the person about it. Just avoid situations in which that person would have influence over you.

Day 16: Peer Pressure

No One Makes Me Do Anything

But each one is tempted when, by his own evil desire, he is dragged away and enticed (James 1:14).

"Don't let your friends talk you into doing something you would be ashamed of, Todd."

"Dad, that whole peer pressure thing is so outdated. No one pressures you into doing anything these days. If anybody offers you anything you don't want, you just say no. That's it. They leave you alone. People respect each other's space."

Todd's dad raised a suspicious eyebrow. "Mm-hm."

"Bye, Dad," Todd said, opening the front door and walking out.

The graduation party had started an hour before and was just getting good when Todd walked in. All his friends were there. The old house was packed like an orange crate with tons of people.

The music was so loud Todd thought the plaster on the walls would crumble any second. This was great. This was going to be fun.

Todd fished his way through the crowd to a corner where he'd spotted several of his buddies. Someone clapped him on the back so hard it stung. It was Gary. He shoved a plastic cup filled with beer into Todd's hand. Beer sloshed out of the cup, soaking the front of Todd's shirt.

Gary smiled a childish grin, seemingly oblivious to what he'd just done.

"Hey, pal," Gary slurred. Todd knew his friend had already had too much, and the night was young. "I've been saving this for ya. Where ya been?"

"Thanks, Gary, but you can keep it." Todd handed the beer back to

Gary, who chugged what was left in one gulp and tossed the empty cup over his shoulder.

"Whatever!" Then he stumbled off through the crowd without even saying good-bye.

Todd didn't feel so comfortable anymore. Leaning against a nearby wall, his eyes roamed the room. Nearly everyone had a beer cup in his or her hand. Where had all that alcohol come from anyway? They were all minors. Several friends walked by, all with a beer. They waved, and he nodded in return. He suddenly felt alone.

Sitting on the shelf next to him was a cup half full of beer. He picked it up. Some of the tensions subsided.

Todd stayed at the party for another hour, the entire time with the half-full cup in his hand. Before he left, he sat it back on the shelf he'd picked it up from, still with the same amount of beer.

"How'd the party go?" Todd's father asked when he walked through the door.

"OK. I was tired, so I came home early. And no, I didn't drink a drop."

"I didn't ask. But thanks for being honest just the same."

Todd offered a half smile and walked up the stairs to his room.

He'd told the truth, but it still didn't stop him from feeling like a liar.

Think About It!

Peer pressure. It affects each of us in many ways. Some have no problems standing up for what they believe. They are the few. Others base their entire self-image upon what others think and say about them. They expend countless hours worrying about whether they're accepted or not. And still others will try to skirt the issues, only acting as if they're going with the masses. No one wants to feel like a loner. Everyone wants to feel loved and accepted. There are two kinds of peer pressure: actual and perceived. Actual peer pressure is when friends actively coerce another friend into doing something, be it good or bad. We've all faced this kind of pressure at sometime or another. But it's actually the lesser seen of the two.

Perceived peer pressure is when everyone else is doing something and we join in just so we won't feel left out. It's the kind of pressure that causes trends to come and go. Perceived peer pressure is far more powerful and widespread than actual. The truth is, however, that perceived peer pressure is usually imagined. Most people don't notice when we spill something all over ourselves. Most people don't notice if we aren't going to the same party as everyone else. Most people don't notice if we don't hang out at the right mall at the right time and shop at the right shops. But the most important thing to remember is, those who do notice don't even care!

Think about it. When we see someone make a fool out of himself or herself, do we even care?

We might have a laugh at first, but then it's over with. When we see our friends talking to people we think aren't the greatest, do we care? Not unless that someone is our most recent ex, and we think our friend's moving in. But by and large, we really don't bat an eye at it.

Negative peer pressure—perceived or actual—is a trick used by Satan to get you to do things you know aren't right. It's easier said than done, but the more we stand up to peer pressure, the better and stronger people we become. We shouldn't buy into everything just because "everyone else is doing it." Three quarters of the people doing it, wish they had the guts not to.

The best thing to do is set our standards and never break them no matter how out of place we feel or how much pressure might come our way. Better for us to stand alone, knowing we did the right thing, than to feel part of the crowd, knowing we broke our word to ourselves and God.

Explore these scriptures:

Feed Your Face

Ps. 91
....

....

....

Rom. 8:31-37

....

....

Acts 4:1-22

....

....

....

Make a pact. Get your Christian friends together. Discuss things you've all struggled with as a result of peer pressure. Sign an agreement to hold each other accountable in these areas. Knowing others agree with you will help you stand firm when pressure sets in.

Ask God for help. In your quiet times, ask God to remind you of your standards. Ask Him to strengthen you as He did the early disciples when they were faced with pressure to stop preaching the gospel.

Day 17: Insults

The Pain of a Put-down

Reckless words pierce like a sword, but the tongue of the wise brings healing (Prov. 12:18).

The jittery 14-year-old swung open the cafeteria doors, scanned the room, then froze. A sharp, sickening pain jabbed at the pit of his stomach.

Day after day, the same thing, Jeremy thought. *I just can't handle this garbage anymore.*

It wasn't the strange cafeteria smells that made him queasy. Jeremy knew he was about to face something far worse: the firing squad at the jocks' table.

"Look, it's the geek of the week," blurted a familiar voice.

Jeremy's heart began playing keyboards with his rib cage, and every muscle grew tense. He took a deep breath and stepped into the food line. Suddenly the same, worn-out barrage of painful word bullets began to fly.

"Dork."

"Wimp."

"Pansy."

An apple core smacked Jeremy on the side of his head, and laughter rose from the table. He squeezed shut his eyes. *Why does this stupid line have to go past the jocks' table?* Jeremy asked himself. *And why won't they leave me alone?*

Think About It!

Insults are never harmless. The fact is, they hurt—deeply. Unlike a gunshot or knife wound, cuts, slams, and jabs weaken a person's self-confidence. And these kinds of wounds often don't heal for many years—if ever.

Jeremy isn't just a character we dreamed up. He's a real person who endured real pain. He claims the teasing he received nearly messed up his identity. Check out the rest of his story:

It got to a point where my own friends wouldn't even sit by me during lunch. We'd get to the cafeteria, and they'd conveniently disappear.

So why did the jocks give me such a hard time? I was a sensitive guy, and the girls liked me. Also I was a Christian and didn't cuss or get into trouble. On top of that, I was a musician—not an athlete. In fact, I hated gym. I was the teen who was always picked last.

By the end of my junior high years, I'd begun to think I was weird because I was creative and not athletic. What saved me was the support I got from my parents, my church, and my youth group.

When I entered high school, I mustered up the courage to start a campus Bible study. I thought, OK, if the guys at school have already labeled me "weird," what will I lose by going all the way with my faith?

An amazing thing happened. When I accepted myself and was confident in the person God made me to be, I slowly gained acceptance from others— even from some of the guys who used to tease me.

Do you find yourself slamming other teens—or are you on the receiving end? The Bible has some stinging words about these common-mouth messes, as well as a healing antidote.

Explore these scriptures:

Feed Your Face

Ps. 34:12-18

Luke 6:27-36

James 3:1-12

Be yourself. In the face of sneers, jeers, and put-downs, never try to be someone you're not—or force yourself to do something you can't. God made you an awesome person just as you are. Stand strong in the strengths and talents He gave you.

Understand that you're not weird. It doesn't

matter if you can't play sports very well or you don't have a perfect body. Every day when you get up and look in the mirror, repeat these words: "I'm OK." (Actually, you'll probably want to wash the sleepy gunk out of your eyes first and brush your teeth—then look in the mirror and repeat those words!)

Remind yourself that your circumstances will change. This isn't how things are going to be forever. Your body is changing, and so are your abilities. If you don't like yourself right now, don't lose hope. In a few years you'll find your niche.

Day 18: Dating

Dating and Relating

*Love the Lord your God with all your heart and with all your
soul and with all your mind. This is the first and greatest
commandment (Matt. 22:37-38).*

Jeff took a sip of soda, fidgeted with his french fries, then
looked across the table at Kayla.
"You look great tonight—different
than in school."

"Thanks," Kayla said. "I
bought this sweater yesterday."

"Cool—this is a new shirt too."
Silence.

"Sooooo—have you heard
what's going on at the youth
group party tonight?" Jeff asked.
"Nope. Haven't heard a thing,
but I'm sure it's gonna be fun."

"Yeah." More silence. Jeff's eyes
scanned the restaurant, then
zeroed in on the fries.

"Good food, huh?"

Kayla nodded her head yes and smiled. Jeff popped a few more fries
into his mouth and sat back.

Even more silence.

I wish I knew her better, Jeff thought. *This would be so much easier—I'd know what to talk about. Aauuuugghhh! There's got to be a better
way!*

Think About It!

It can be awkward. It can be nerve-racking.
But that exciting—and often frustrating—human
activity known as dating sets into motion the lifelong challenge of understanding the opposite sex.

It's also the first few steps males and females
take as they pursue a "one person forever" dream;

Someday in the future, when I become an adult, I will find that special person with whom I can share all my secrets for the rest of my life.

FACT: God is the author of this dream.

FACT: God wants it to be fulfilled in a committed, lifelong marriage.

With this in mind, it's not hard to understand why dating can be so hard—and why rejection can chip away at our confidence. (And does all this give you a clue as to why God has designed sex for marriage—not dating?)

So what's the right strategy when it comes to dating? How should you date—and what are the boundaries?

As a teenager, you're beginning to develop a pretty clear vision of who you're becoming and what kind of person your ideal man or woman will be. Now it's time to build your "one person forever" dream deliberately and well. We've filled today's lesson with some important steps that will guard your heart from major attack.

Explore these scriptures:

Feed Your Face

1 Cor. 13:6

Eph. 5:1-2

1 Thess. 4:3-5

Define dating. At this stage in your life, dating should be defined as "having fun getting to know the opposite sex," not "discovering how far I can go sexually." Your focus should be on fun, not romance. (We'll say it again: God created sex for marriage, not dating.)

Pray often—especially about the kinds of people you are planning to go out with. Honor Jesus Christ with your social life and live "worthy of the calling you have received" (Eph. 4:1). Be sure your attitude and actions reflect God's standards. And whenever you detect a selfish desire as you date—such as infatuation with lust instead of godly love—turn it over to the Lord.

Shape up! Your maturity is being shaped as you take responsibility with matters of the heart. What's more, the pleasures of intimacy are so strong and so appealing that they test your responsibility as no other life experience does. Choosing to stay pure and to obey God with your dating life results in some solid benefits:

-You'll grow spiritually, mentally, emotionally, and socially.

-You'll be better prepared for the responsibilities of marriage.

-You'll grow into the kind of person your future mate needs.

Focus on your true Love. The One who created you cares about you—and loves you just as you are. In fact, God loves you beyond what you can even imagine love to be. And He has an awesome plan for your life. Be patient and depend on Him. Most importantly, put Him first and love Him "with all your heart and with all your soul and with all your mind" (Matt. 22:37).

Day 19: Sex — *Is Cupid Stupid?*

It is God's will that you should be sanctified: that you should avoid sexual immorality; that each of you should learn to control his own body in a way that is holy and honorable, not in passionate lust like the heathen, who do not know God (1 Thess. 4:3-5).

"Why would God give us a desire for sex, then tell us to wait until marriage to experience it?"

Cheryl's remark struck a nerve with the other girls in her Bible study group.

"I don't get it either," Jill chimed in. "And where does the Bible actually say to *wait until marriage?*"

Annette's eyes lit up as she thumbed through some passages. "Hey, listen to this about a Bible hero," she said sarcastically, then began reading the story about David and Bathsheba. "'From the roof he saw a woman bathing. . . . She came to him, and he slept with her'" (2 Sam. 11:2, 4).

"Sounds like the ancient people of the faith didn't always follow the rules," Cheryl said. "And they're supposed to be our role models!"

Jennifer, who was sitting alone in a corner of Cheryl's bedroom, looked up in disbelief. *They're totally missing the point,* she thought. *They're twisting what the Bible really says.* A stabbing pain shot through her stomach, but what she heard next nearly made her blood boil.

Cheryl hugged her pillow, smiled, then leaned closer to the other girls. "I'll let you in on a secret," she said. "But you can't tell anyone."

"I gotta hear this," Jill said.

"Gary and I have decided that it's time to . . . you know," Cheryl said sheepishly. "He has protection, and he's conveniently bringing it to the senior high ski retreat next weekend."

"You mean the annual 'Make-Out Fest'!" Jill said with a laugh.

"I think if you two love each other," Annette added, "then it's right. I know I'm not waiting until marriage. That could be *forever!*"

Cheryl locked eyes with Jennifer. "So what do you think?"

"Yeah, you've been quiet all evening—speak up," Annette barked.

Jennifer looked back at Cheryl and swallowed. "OK, you asked, so I'll be honest with you," she said. "Sex between two people who aren't married to each other is wrong. The Bible is clear about sex—and lots of other stuff."

Jennifer fidgeted with her bracelet, searching for the right words. "I mean, why read this Book and have weekly studies if you don't believe what it says? If you really want to live for God, then you've got to focus on His truth—not what seems right at the moment."

The room was completely silent. Jennifer couldn't believe what just came out of her mouth. *Thanks, Lord, but now they think I'm a Bible thumper—and they'll probably never talk to me again. Please, get me out of this one. Show me what else to say.*

Think About It! **Why didn't God make waiting for sex easier?** Why didn't He just give us sexual desires on our wedding night—and not a moment before? These are tough questions with no simple answers.

But despite the mixed messages you hear on television or from friends, here's the truth: God designed sex to be enjoyed in marriage—between a husband and wife who are committed to each other for life.

Unlike any other experience between a married couple, sexual intercourse creates the deepest, most powerful bond that is never supposed to be separated. Sex involves a couple's bodies, minds, and emotions in an activity that is intended to continue for a lifetime.

Sex before marriage—sex without complete commitment—is like dessert before the meal. It could spoil our appetite for really healthy food. People who have sex without commitment usually never get to the commitment. People who try sex without marriage find it hard to create lasting, loving relationships.

Explore these scriptures:

Feed Your Face

Lev. 18:1-30

1 Cor. 6:12-20

2 Tim. 2:14-26

Save your heart from major attack. Make this commitment to God: "I'm saving myself for marriage."

Stand firm—even when the pressure makes you squirm. Never buy the lie that "sex will help us really get to know each other." People who say stuff like that usually don't care about the other person or being intimate. What they really want is sex. And most guys and girls who give in find themselves alone.

Understand that sex isn't just "recreation." Some teens reduce sex to a physical act and just another way of having fun. Be different. Let others know you hold sex in high regard and don't want to cheapen this wonderful gift by giving it away to just anyone. Don't be afraid to tell others, "I'm saving it for that special person who'll be my partner for life."

Seek God's best. Every person on this planet shares a need to love and to be loved. And as those who follow Christ deepen their faith, they learn that the foundation of love must come from a committed relationship with Jesus. Remember—the Lord hasn't given us meaningless guidelines in order to make life boring. His timeless instructions are intended to protect us from harm and to insure that we get the most out of the gifts He provides—like sex.

Entrust your future marriage to God. Understand now that when you feel ready for marriage—which is probably several years down the road—it may take a period of patient waiting before God speaks to you about this issue. We must be willing to listen to Him patiently because these times may be necessary to stretch our faith. He has promised to speak to our hearts, so we can expect Him to, but He is not compelled to tell us everything we want to know the moment we desire the information.

Day 20: Peer Evangelism
It Takes Guts!

He said to them, "Go into all the world and preach the good news to all creation" (Mark 16:15).

Todd sat across the table from Shilo every day in study hall. Today, Shilo had his headset on and the music turned up so loud that everyone around him could hear it too. The wail of guitars cut through the silent room distinctly. Shilo's long, unwashed hair swung rhythmically as he bobbed his head up and down. He was totally oblivious to everything.

Todd watched, amazed. Intimidation was not something Todd usually experienced. But this was different. He was certain Shilo

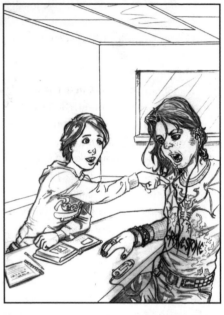

bordered on the psychotic. He'd heard two seniors say so yesterday in the lunchroom.

"Mmm! Hmmm hmmm!" Shilo hummed the lyrics loudly, indifferent as to whether he disturbed anyone. "Hmm mmm! . . . Jesus Christ! . . . Mmmm! Like the wimp he was! . . ."

Todd's curiosity peaked. He had to know what Shilo was listening to. Shilo was a self-proclaimed atheist according to most people. Todd thought the only time Shilo said "Jesus Christ" was as a swear word.

Todd tapped on the table in front of Shilo with his pencil. His gut wrenched when Shilo's head snapped up, staring daggers through him with bloodshot eyes rimmed with black mascara. With a sheepish smile, Todd tapped his ears indicating the headset.

"What?" Shilo snarled, pulling the headset away from his ears just enough to hear what the rude interruption concerned.

"What'cha listening to?"

Shilo chewed on the question for several long seconds as if it was a riddle to be solved.

"Why?" He removed the earphones, tossed them on the table, and pushed the pause button on his MP3 player.

"Curious is all," Todd said, swallowing hard. This was the most he'd talked to the guy across the table from him, ever. "I heard you say 'Jesus Christ,' and I wanted to know what song it was."

"It's just a lyric, man. No big deal."

Todd slid his tongue across the bridge of his mouth and puckered his lips in thought. "It's more than that to me."

Shilo raised an eyebrow at him. "How so?"

"Jesus died on a cross 2,000 years ago, not because He had to but because He wanted to. He wasn't a wimp. He died willingly because He loved humanity more than anything. Then after He died He came back to life again three days later and conquered death—all because He wanted to give you and me eternal life."

Shilo stared at Todd absentmindedly as if he couldn't believe what he was hearing. "Small words from someone who believes in fairy tales," he eventually said.

"Truth is often stranger than fiction. But this isn't a fairy tale. It really did happen."

Shilo snatched the headset off the table and stood up, eyeing Todd like a cat. "You're weird." He placed the earphones around his head, stabbed the play button, and stalked off.

Todd smiled as he watched Shilo leaving.

You can't catch 'em all.

Think About It! **Jesus challenged us to share the gospel with the whole world.** Given time, He'll provide all the opportunities to share that we can handle. It's not an option. It's an obligation.

God didn't give us the gift of life to keep it to ourselves. The world is dying. If we don't share Jesus with them, how will they ever come to know Him?

Sharing Jesus doesn't mean we have to deliver a sermon. You don't have to stand on a street corner declaring the coming of the end of the world and then offer hope to those you can pin down. It can be as simple as telling your friends what Jesus did for you and what life as a Christian means. It doesn't have to be confrontational or militaristic. In fact, that approach turns more people away than not.

Jesus didn't take that approach. He simply showed love to people, built a bridge to them, met their needs, and then told them what God was all about. If they weren't ready for it, He didn't badger them. He simply let it drop; confident He had done the best He could.

We should take the same approach: build bridges and friendships with as many people as we can—show them there's something different about us. But when the opportunity arises for us to share Jesus (don't worry—it will), we should take advantage of it without shame.

They may not break down in tears and beg us to lead them to the Cross, but you never know. The gospel has more power and appeal than we give it credit for. Anything could happen.

Explore these scriptures:

Feed Your Face

Phil. 1:12-18

Rom. 12:13-17

Acts 2:29-42

Don't be shy. Always be on the lookout for the chance to get a word in about Jesus. It may sound outrageous, but the happiest people are often those who can't keep their mouths shut about what Jesus has done for them. Besides, it's not something to be ashamed of. Stand up and be counted!

Develop a system. Know what to say in case you're confronted and someone wants you to lead him or her to the Lord. Talk with your pastor or youth leader. See what approach he or she uses.

A good plan is one that is scripturally based and explains to the seeker what's happening.

Follow-up is key. After you lead someone to the Lord, don't leave the new believer hanging. Invite the person to church and get him or her in a discipleship program or started immediately on a path to learning what God is all about. If you can afford it and if the person needs one, provide him or her with a Bible. You might want to get some reading material that will help the person develop a quiet time (we suggest a copy of this book—but then, we're biased). But by all means, don't leave the new Christian to flounder.

Day 21: Loyalty
Don't Take Part

Let your conversation be always full of grace, seasoned with salt, so that you may know how to answer everyone (Col. 4:6).

Beth straightened her blouse and cleared her throat. No one seemed to notice. She picked up a magazine from the coffee table and thumbed through it. She tried to not even listen to the three other girls' conversation, but it was difficult not to hear what was being said. For the last hour Cassidy, Amy, and Tamarra had laughed at, talked about, and ridiculed every other girl in their youth group.

Beth had come over at their invitation, thinking they would all be going to the mall shortly after she arrived. When she walked in, there was the usual small talk about school and guys. But as the conversation continued, the small talk turned into hateful gossip. Beth couldn't believe her ears. These girls claimed to be Christians?

Cassidy and Amy had even stood up and testified the week before during youth group. In tears they had each shared how they "love everyone in the group so much" and declared, "I don't know what I'd do without them." What Beth heard now sure didn't sound much like love. *If the youth group knew what was being said about them* . . . Beth shuddered to think of it. The three were all considered trusted leaders and confidants of the youth group.

I wonder what they say about me when I'm not around, she thought.

She hadn't said a word since the conversation went sour. All she wanted to do was get out of there. The sooner the better. She wanted the horrible gossiping to end more than anything, but she felt helpless to stop it.

"What do you think, Beth? You've hardly said anything since you walked in."

"Oh, sorry. I wasn't paying attention. What were you saying?" Beth dropped the magazine to her lap, contemplating what to say next.

"We were talking about Sarah. Cassidy says she's too sweet to be real," Tamarra snickered. "I think I agree. No one's that candy coated."

Beth almost choked. Sarah was her best friend and the kindest person she knew. She struggled to control her temper, honestly wanting nothing more than to lash out at these so-called friends.

"What I think," Beth said as she slowly stood up, "is that I'm not going to be a part of this conversation anymore. You all know how you hate it when people talk about you behind your backs—what makes you think it's any different when you do it?"

She looked at her three friends and continued. "Just because we're Christians doesn't make gossiping any less wrong. We've just spent the last hour running everyone into the ground; I just don't believe this type of conversation is healthy—not for us or for our relationship with our friends. Or with God."

On that note, Beth gathered her purse and keys and walked out of the house, her three friends still staring at the front door as she drove away.

Think About It!

Research seems to indicate that not many people in today's society can really be trusted. Surveys show the vast majority of society thinks nothing about telling a lie if it will benefit them in the end. Many people don't even know if they have any true friends. Cheating, lying, and self-centeredness have turned us into a nation that can't be trusted. What a sad statement about our world!

In the old West, a man's word was his contract. Now lawyers scoff at verbal contracts as nonbinding nonsense. It hardly even fazes us to see people talking behind each other's backs one minute and making plans to go do something together the next.

Loyalty has almost no definition in this generation. Mistrust, abandonment, and exploitation are so common we don't expect much from each other. *Why should we? If we do, we'll only be hurt again.*

God calls us to break that pattern. Among Christians there's no room for tearing each other down. There's too much work to be done in the Kingdom. Lying, cheating, gossiping, and backbiting only create division in God's family. The example Christ gave us was remarkable—to stand by us even if it meant His life. And that's exactly what it cost Him. To call ourselves Christians and then act as though we aren't cheapens the price Jesus paid. Better to put those activities behind us and find out what true loyalty is all about.

Explore these scriptures:

Feed Your Face

Rom. 15:1-7

Acts 2:42-47

2 Tim. 2:22-26

Pay the price. Want to teach yourself not to gossip or put others down? Charge yourself a quarter every time you catch yourself doing it. Give it to your youth pastor, your parents, or a trusted friend. Make sure you're completely honest about it too. After they've collected enough from you to buy a new pair of jeans, you'll get the idea.

Humble yourself. Build up as much courage as you can. Then go to someone you've talked badly about and apologize, even if they didn't know you had been talking about them. You'll be surprised at the reaction you get and the joy and relief you'll feel inside.

Tales from the *Grind*

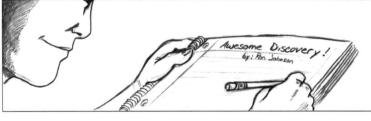

SECTION 4
LIFE AT HOME

Casting Your Cares

Do you feel as if your life is in a cast? Are problems at home making you wonder if God really cares about you?

No doubt Ron experienced more pain than most people endure in a lifetime, yet this teen, along with his girlfriend, made an awesome discovery: Despite the storms we encounter in life, God never leaves us. Even though we're weak, He is able.

This week let's turn our hearts toward home.

Wake-Up Call
Weekly Bible Study

● List the top 10 things that really bug you about your family.

1. ....

2. ....

3. ....

4. ....

5. ....

6. ....

7. ....

8. ....

9. ....

10. ....

● From this list, name the biggest issue you and your family fight about.

....

....

● What are some steps you can take to solve this problem?

....

....

....

● Read Genesis 37:1-11.
Why do you suppose Joseph's brothers hated him so much?
What mistakes did his father make?

● Read Genesis 37:12-36.
List how Joseph probably felt as he sat alone in the bottom of a well.
(We've even helped you out with a few words.)

❏ Abandoned

❏ Confused

❏

❏

❏

❏

❏

❏

Had God left him at that moment? (Why do you think God let him endure this kind of pain?)

● Let's skip ahead to Genesis 45. Read verses 1-15.
Why do you think Joseph forgave his brothers?
If a family member had done something equally bad to you, could you forgive him or her? Why or why not?

● Question: Why do you think some parents tend to overprotect their children—sometimes to the point of alienating them?
For a clue, consider this possibility: It's likely that some mothers and fathers did not get enough nurturing when they were children, or the

kind of parenting they needed. So they vowed long ago to make life better for their own children—never letting them feel neglected.

Does this comment apply to you? Why or why not?
Do you feel as if your parents "love you too much"?
Do your parents view you as an extension of themselves?
What can you do to promote healthy personal boundaries or private space?

● Of the following messages you need to hear from Mom and Dad, which is the most important to you? Why?
    "I love you."
    "I'm proud of you."
    "I trust you."
    "I'll never reject you."

● What do you want Mom and Dad to know about you? Write out anything you'd like. Hey—you won't get grounded!

● Now list the top 10 things you really like about your family.

    1. ....

    2. ....

    3. ....

    4. ....

    5. ....

    6. ....

    7. ....

    8. ....

    9. ....

    10. ....

● What can you do to help make life better for your family?

● This week launch Operation Care for My Family.

First, talk to God. Pour out your heart about stuff at home that's really bugging you, as well as stuff you're thankful for. Ask the Lord for direction and a way to improve life in your home.

Second, schedule a talk session. Get alone with Mom or Dad (or both) and share what's on your heart. (Tell them it's an assignment from your devotion book!)

Third, pick one of the projects listed below and carry it out. (Which activities are you going to pick—and why?)

Write your parents a letter, telling them how much you appreciate them.

Prepare any food item the family would enjoy. (Mom loves it any-time she doesn't have to cook!)

Make a card (even just a note with a handwritten "I love you" on it).

Buy a plant, a flower, or a scripture plaque for the wall, and give it to your parents.

Give an "IOU" note to do something together that Mom or Dad likes (even though you may not)—a walk, or a Sunday afternoon drive, for example.

Make up a coupon book that might include cleaning up the dishes or the house, a kiss on the cheek, a hug, a cup of tea, an errand, breakfast in bed, a car wash, or baby-sitting.

Day 22: Family Life
Why God Invented the Family

*God sets the lonely in families . . . but the rebellious live in a
sun-scorched land (Ps. 68:6)*

A long time ago in a galaxy far, far away, God created an odd and highly temperamental species known as—*the parent*. And because God loved this creation, He decided to place it in a very special environment known as—*the family unit*. Then one day, God decided to bless the parent and the family unit with perhaps His greatest of all creations, an equally odd and highly temperamental species known as—*the teenager*.

And even though God looked upon His creation and said, "It is good," many teenagers and parents through the ages have scratched their heads and asked the eternally mysterious question:

What was God thinking?

Think About It!

If you were asked to take a survey on family life, it's not too difficult to figure out how you'd rate your home:

My family is best described as
  a. the Brady Bunch
  b. the Simpsons
  c. the Osbornes
  d. fill in the blank

Like most teens, you'd probably choose d. fill in the blank—and you'd write something like "a loony bin, an insane asylum, a madhouse."

Face it: life on the home front is sometimes hard. Yet despite how strange it can be with your family, the good news is:

There *isn't* a computer chip inside Mom and Dad's head that's programmed to ruin your life.

Your pesky little brother *isn't* a mutant Neanderthal kid who escaped from the circus.

Your older sister doesn't spend all that time in the bathroom perfecting her plot for world domination.

God *didn't* make a mistake.

While no family on the face of this earth is perfect, every family is very important—especially to God. Whether you realize it or not, your family is teaching you how to get along with other people and is actually helping you to smooth out your rough edges. In fact, God designed your home as a place where you can:

1. *grow* and *develop* into the kind of person He designed you to be
2. learn how to someday *grow* your own family
3. have a safe place in which to *grow* closer to Him

Explore these scriptures:

Feed Your Face

Col. 3:18-25

Prov. 13:1

1 Tim. 5:8

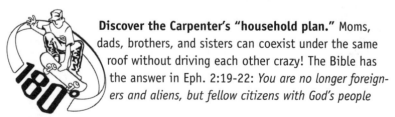

Discover the Carpenter's "household plan." Moms, dads, brothers, and sisters can coexist under the same roof without driving each other crazy! The Bible has the answer in Eph. 2:19-22: *You are no longer foreigners and aliens, but fellow citizens with God's people*

and members of God's household, built on the foundation of the apostles and prophets, with Christ Jesus himself as the chief cornerstone. In him the whole building is joined together and rises to become a holy temple in the Lord. And in him you too are being built together to become a dwelling in which God lives by his Spirit.

Memorize the passage above and ask God to help you and your family become a dwelling place for His Holy Spirit.

Strive to be a peacemaker. How? For a clue, check out Eph. 4:1-3: *As a prisoner for the Lord, then, I urge you to live a life worthy of the calling you have received. Be completely humble and gentle; be patient, bearing with one another in love. Make every effort to keep the unity of the Spirit through the bond of peace.*

Follow this three-point strategy to handling home-front hassles: (1) Commit your life to the Lord, turn away from sin, and seek God for answers. (2) Understand that no problem is too big for God to handle— not even a fight with Mom or Dad. God will set you on the right course if you let Him. (3) Seek unity and solutions to problems, not strife and pointless quarrels.

Day 23: Changing Families

Modern Problems

> He will turn the hearts of the fathers to their children, and the hearts of the children to their fathers; or else I will come and strike the land with a curse (Mal. 4:6).

Tina hustles into Mrs. Stephen's first-period English class seconds before the door is shut. She flashes a grin at a friend, then takes her seat in the last desk of the last row. On the outside, Tina looks like a typical teen. But the inside's another story. During class she writes in her journal:

I feel like I'm in a dark, cold prison cell. It's really scary, because the walls are closing in and there's no way out. What's the use of going on?

Mom and Dad never have time for the family—or for each other. And when I see them, they're always fighting about bills and money and work . . . and about not having enough time for anything. I even heard them talk about getting a divorce.

My older brother headed off to college—and right into the gay lifestyle. He said he won't tolerate us "narrow-minded Christian hypocrites" until we accept his "true identity."

My little sister is so freaked out about everything she spends all of her time on the Internet. I don't think she knows what it's like to talk to a real person. But, hey, at least she isn't walking in her big sister's footsteps and numbing the anger with an occasional pill from

Mom's medicine cabinet . . . or a few shots of Jack Daniels from Dad's liquor stash.

Everything's falling apart. I just can't go on.

Tina scribbled one last line in her journal: *If this is how a family is supposed to be, then I don't want to live in one anymore.*

Think About It! **Does Tina's crisis hit home?** We live in a mixed-up world of high-tech toys and low-tech values, and it's taking a toll on many families. Too many households—including Christian ones—have tuned in the voices of today's self-centered, greed-and-trash culture and tuned out the ultimate Truth—Jesus Christ.

Take a look at three major modern problems some families face:

Loss of leadership. An intact family of a husband and wife who display a loving, giving, respectful relationship provides a model and a standard for you to follow. But just who runs today's busy families? It isn't too clear sometimes. A number of dads are missing from the home—either because of divorce or demanding careers. And because moms are now as commonplace in today's workforce as dads, this leaves the kids at home alone to call the shots. *Who gets hurt? Teens like you.*

Materialism has replaced values. "Show me the money" is the philosophy of our times. Ask your friends what future goal is most important to them, and they respond, "A high-paying job so I can buy what I want and live the way I want." And guess what? Your peers are growing up to be moms and dads who are motivated by materialism. *Who gets hurt? Teens like you.*

Divorce is commonplace. It has been said that "each divorce is the death of a small civilization." Can you see how the breakup of the family unit can eventually destroy a nation? Since the early 1980s, the percentage of marriages ending in divorce has held steady between 40-50 percent.[1] Let's assume there are at least a million marriages that take place each year. Over a ten year span there will be approximately five million divorces that take place. Statistically speaking, the average family has approximately 2.5 kids. That means a whole lot of kids will witness their parents' marriage break up before and during their teenage years. *Who gets hurt? Teens like you.* Many teens from broken homes feel overwhelming stress, including a deep sense of abandonment, or a feeling of responsibility for the divorce—scars they end up carrying into adulthood.

Family life can be the closest thing to heaven on earth if we follow God's plan. It can also be the closest thing to hell. It's a choice every member of the family takes part in.

The key is demonstrating mutual respect out of a heart of love for God. Your family can be strong and wonderful if everyone in your house would take God's standards seriously and commit your hearts to each other—and to Him.

True, some situations are out of your control, but there's a lot you can do to help make your home a better place.

Explore these scriptures:

Feed Your Face

Ps. 27:10-14

Mark 10:9

Eph. 5:21-33

Have a pull-together-not-apart attitude. When your little brother comes to you for help—regardless of how pesky he may seem—don't shove him away. Instead, reach out to him. And when Mom and Dad ask you to do something, don't complain. Do what they ask.

Learn to live for others. It's easy to be selfish and to think that the world revolves around you, including your family. But family unity is strengthened when each member thinks about the needs of others—not themselves. Plus, a cooperative attitude may increase the chances of your parents giving you more privileges in the future.

Be in the world, not of it. Just because you live in a self-centered, greed-and-trash culture, you don't have to buy its lies or contribute to it. Focus on what God wants from you, not on what the world says you should have. Begin with a very basic principle God wants you to act upon: *Love the Lord your God with all your heart and with all your soul and with all your mind* (Matt. 22:37).

Day 24: Hassles
Home-Front Hotspots

Flee the evil desires of youth, and pursue righteousness, faith, love and peace. . . . Don't have anything to do with foolish and stupid arguments, because you know they produce quarrels (2 Tim. 2:22-23).

Suddenly, from out of nowhere, you hear the theme song from that '70s movie *Jaws*: "DAH, DAH . . . DAH, DAH . . . DAH, DAH . . ."

Just when you thought it was safe to surface from your room—*bam!*—you have a head-on collision with your mom.

"Do your chores and clean your room. And don't forget to finish your homework. And put something else on—you can't go out looking like that. Don't roll your eyes at me."

Double bam! Dad thunders around the corner. "Where do you think you're going? Your mother and I don't approve of your friends. You need to stay home more and stop spending money. Do I look like a bank?"

Quick! Escape out the front door. *Aaaurrrggg!* It's locked. You casually retreat to your room and wait for the coast to clear. You pull on your headphones and punch up your latest tunes on your MP3 player.

"God, help me" you mumble. *"Mom and Dad are on the warpath—and I feel like I'm their prime target!"*

Think About It!

"My parents are always on my case."

"My parents don't trust me."

"My parents play favorites—and pick on me."

Familiar complaints? Actually these three statements rank high on most teens' top 10 list of hassles. And if you feel as though you're on your parents' most wanted list, you're probably right. Regardless of all the home-front hotspots you encounter, it's safe to say that you really are wanted by your mom and dad and they really do love you. It's just at times they may have trouble expressing their love. (Come to think of it, you're not always able to express your love either.)

What's more, it's hard for some parents to accept that you're growing up, and don't need as much care now as you did when you were a helpless baby. At the same time, some teens just aren't ready for more freedom. They still act like—well, helpless babies. How about you? Are you giving your parents a reason to get off your case and to start trusting you more, or are you giving them a reason to go on the warpath?

Raising a teen like you is an awesome responsibility. God has given your parents a five-part job description: It's up to them to protect you, train you, provide for you, nurture you toward maturity, and discipline you. And God has given you a job description too. It's your job to obey them (see Eph. 6:1) and minimize the "foolish and stupid arguments" (reread 2 Tim. 2:22-23).

Explore these scriptures:

Feed Your Face

Gen. 18:19

Deut. 6:6-7

Heb. 12:8-10

Understand the battle. As a teenager, you're very sensitive about personal injustice, self-worth, independence, privacy, and love. And whether or not you admit it, you're actually looking for boundaries. Some of your testing behaviors are a way of you saying, *Do you care enough about me to keep me from doing this stupid thing? Do I have your attention? Are you concerned about who I am and what I'm doing?*

Think through the conflict. The next time you have a head-on collision with your parents, ask yourself a few questions: Why are they acting this way? Have I done something wrong, or are they just tired? Am I behaving the right way, or am I making matters worse?

Get to the root of a problem. Understand that when two people have trouble getting along, it's usually because a problem has built up over time. So if trust is the hot-button issue, talk with your parents and get to the root of why they don't trust you. Then, together, set some new ground rules, vow to make a change, and set off on the right foot.

Show respect. Guess what? When you show respect to your parents, you'll get it back. Not only will they return it, but they'll begin to trust you more.

Day 25: Independence

Every Teen's Battle

Children, obey your parents in the Lord, for this is right. "Honor your father and mother" (Eph. 6:1-2).

It happened again—another Tuesday night fight. This time with Mom. Brandon flops on his bed and bounces a basketball against his Pacers poster.

"'No-o-o-o-o,'" he mumbles in his best prison-warden voice. "'You can't have that, you can't go there, you can't hang out with those friends!' Does she think I still wear Pampers? When will she learn I'm not a little kid anymore?"

Then his mind flashes to his buddy at youth group. Todd doesn't even have a mom. (She died a few years back.) And his dad works so hard at the office they barely see each other.

At first, Brandon thought Todd had it made—with all the freedom a teen could want. Then Todd surprised Brandon with what he said at retreat last winter: "Sure it's a pain when moms nag you about stuff . . . but I'd give anything to get mine back. She always did a million little things to show how much she loved me. I really loved her too. If she were still alive, I wouldn't let a day pass without telling her that."

Suddenly Brandon feels lower than a snake's belly in a wagon rut. OK, so Mom isn't a prison warden, and I shouldn't have acted like a jerk. But she and Dad are always on my case about stuff. Why can't they cut me some slack and let me make my own decisions?

Think About It! **How is it possible to love people so much, yet at times feel as if you can't stand them?** How can you live under the same roof with your mom, dad, brother, and sister—be so close to them, know all of their strange quirks—yet feel as if they're the biggest strangers you've ever met?

There's only one place that can bring out all these conflicting emotions—*your family*. Whether you like it or not, an emotional war has erupted between you and your parents—one that started when you became a teenager. Don't panic because it's perfectly normal. Nearly every teen and parent experiences this phase that psychologists describe as the war of independence. With each step you take on the path to adulthood, you become more and more independent of your parents.

Someday you will be on your own, free to make your own decisions and choices. But in the meantime, how can you survive the daily storms on your home front, and even improve your relationship with your family?

Explore these scriptures:

Feed Your Face

Luke 15:11-32

Eph. 4:29—5:2

Col. 3:18-21

Don't shut down or put up a 10-foot-thick wall between you and your parents. This creates more tension between you and them. Instead, make an effort to talk to your parents about stuff that bugs you—as well as what's going on in your life. As you'll discover in the next few lessons, making an effort to communicate and to listen will ultimately open the doors to greater understanding.

Ask your parents to trust you with small decisions. "After all, how else can I learn to recover from bad choices?" you can point out. "Let me learn plenty on the small stuff so I can avoid the cost of messing up on the big stuff." But remember: Trust is a two-way street. *Gaining* your parents' trust means being *worthy* of their trust.

Ask for space. Explain that every person—especially a teenager— needs escape from authority figures to reflect, think, make plans, communicate with God—alone.

Follow Christ's example. The Bible mentions only one event from Jesus' growing-up years. (Open your Bible again and read Luke 2:41-52.) When He was 12, He went to the Temple with His parents. When His mother and father decided to head home, they assumed Jesus was following them. Suddenly, they discovered that He was missing. The frightened parents rushed back to the Temple and three days later found Jesus calmly talking with the scholars. "Son, why have you treated us like this?" Mary asked. Note Jesus' reaction. He didn't sulk or lose His temper. Instead, He obeyed His parents and went with them. Jesus obviously understood the war of independence.

Day 26: Listening
Can You Hear Me?

Everyone should be quick to listen, slow to speak and slow to become angry, for man's anger does not bring about the righteous life that God desires (James 1:19-20).

Conversation No. 1—How It Could Be . . .

Teen: I hate my English Composition class, and I don't see the point in taking it. It's not like I'm gonna be a novelist someday.

Parent: I hear you—writing can be hard. But you know, I'm glad I stuck with it when I was your age. Is there any way I can help?

Teen: You actually understand what I'm going through—cool! I have to write a two-page theme paper tonight. Got any suggestions for a topic?

Parent: Have a seat, and let's see what we can dream up together.

Teen: Thanks. This really takes a load off my mind.

Conversation No. 2—How It Often Is . . .

Teen: I hate my English Composition class, and I don't see the point in taking it. It's not like I'm gonna be a novelist someday.

Parent: You might not become a novelist, but you'll at least need to know how to communicate effectively on paper no matter what profession you choose. Besides, English is a requirement, so you need to get to work on your homework.

Teen: Yeah, well I don't care if I flunk it so I think I'll skip the homework.

Parent: I don't appreciate your tone or your attitude. Get to work on your homework—now!

Teen: You never listen to me when I have a problem. I can't wait till I'm on my own and don't have to put up with your stupid rules.

Parent: Keep it up, Smart Mouth, and you'll get yourself grounded.

Teen: This stinks. You're ruining my life.

Think About It! **So which conversation is typical in your house?** The second one? Too bad because Conversation No. 1 isn't that far out of touch with reality. In fact, with some work it can actually be the regular mode of conversation. But it all begins with an important nine-letter word: listening.

Listening is where effective communication really begins. The best communication tool God gave us is not our lips but our ears.

OK, we know what you're thinking: My parents are the problem. They just don't give me a chance. And they never listen!

You may be right. Your parents probably don't listen to you as much as you'd like. But it's also safe to say that you don't listen to them or give them a chance. Instead, you find yourself in a verbal tug-of-war.

If you're like most teens, you want to communicate with your parents, but you just don't know where to begin. If you're willing to ask the right questions—and listen to your parents' answers—you'll have a place to start.

Explore these scriptures:

Feed Your Face Prov. 18:1-13

117

John 10:25-30

James 1:19-27

During a confrontation, ask a simple, caring question—then listen to the response. That's what one fed-up teen did. At a morning church service the pastor preached about how important it is for families to spend time together. He explained that parents need to spend time alone with each child every day, suggesting that they go for walks or out to dinner or just stay home and play a game.

The message had touched a nerve with the teen. He felt neglected by his dad and wanted to set things right. So after the service the teen took his dad aside and told him how badly he wanted the family to spend more time together—as long as everyone also got a healthy dose of space from time to time. Then the teen asked, "How do you feel about what the pastor said?"

"I liked every word," his dad responded. "But I feel we connect pretty well—and spend lots of time together. Do you disagree?"

Suddenly the boy had his dad's full attention—as well as his chance to finally be heard. "You haven't done any of the things the pastor mentioned since I was a little boy," he explained. "At times I feel neglected. All you do is work, and that makes me wonder if you really love me. I want us to spend more time together. I especially need you to listen to me—and really hear what's going on in my life."

In the weeks that followed, the boy ended up getting what he'd asked for, and life in his household improved greatly.

Unlock the door to effective listening. Follow these essential steps, and try putting them into practice with your parents.

1. **Begin with passive listening (or silence).** Give your parents a chance to speak. Give acknowledging responses. Don't just stand there with a blank expression on your face. Even when you're listening passively, it's a good idea to make sincere comments such as "I see" or "Oh?" that emphasize that you're paying attention.

2. **Offer a door opener.** A door opener is a simple, nonjudgmental statement such as "I was wondering how you feel about me going out with my friends instead of joining you guys for family night." Such a simple invitation may feel awkward, but rest assured "How you feel"-type questions are less threatening to your parents, and they help spark communication.

3. **Exercise active listening.** Try restating what your parents just told you without losing your cool or popping off with a rude remark. Go back and compare Conversation No. 1 to Conversation No. 2. Notice how the responses from both parent and teen are more positive and open the door to communication.

Day 27: Communication
How to Speak Parent-ese

Before a word is on my tongue you know it completely, O LORD (Ps. 139:4).

It's Tuesday night, and Jennifer and her mom are in a heated discussion about how late she can stay out Friday. Suddenly Jennifer pops off with a stinging remark— "You never care about what I want; you're just out to drive me crazy all the time!"—followed by a long list of gripes, like the time when she was a toddler and her mom took away her favorite squeaky toy, and then made her eat strained asparagus.

At this point, the mother and daughter are full-tilt steamed— and nothing's getting resolved.

Think About It! **Tired of pointless arguments with Mom and Dad that seem to get nowhere**—except maybe with your being grounded? Good communication, along with a strong desire to improve life in your home, is the answer. And by learning how to connect with your parents and express your point, you'll have a better chance of getting what you want.

It's not just the trying that's important, you really have to want it too—not just so you can get your way, but because you respect your parents. Sure, there are those situations where parents aren't the best of role models and really can make every moment difficult. But by and large, most parents don't want to argue with their kids all the time. They want to communicate effectively.

The scary issue is that if you don't learn how to communicate successfully at least during your teen years, then this problem will in all likelihood carry on into your adult life. Good communication is key to any relationship you'll be placed in. If you don't conquer this skill early on, then you will probably struggle with friendships and love relationships the rest of your life.

The bottom line: With determination and practice, your communication skills will improve. Remember, good communication keeps doors open, but bad communication may end up getting your door shut and locked.

Explore these scriptures:

Feed Your Face

Prov. 15:1-7

Eph. 4:29—5:2

1 Thess. 5:12-22

KEY 1: Attitude is everything. When Mom and Dad tick you off, never—I repeat—never fire back with an angry remark. (That's what gets you sent to your cell . . . uh . . . we mean room.) This only raises defenses and widens the gap. A controlled temper and respectful tone allow for a better chance at conflict resolution.

KEY 2: Stay away from blanket statements. Phrases like "you never" and "you always" sound accusatory and cause the listener to become defensive. Instead, stress your particular wants and feelings by using "I." For example, saying "I want" or "I feel" are effective places to begin.

KEY 3: Maintain eye contact. Maintaining eye contact can be hard, especially when you're upset. But looking away or ignoring your parents when they're trying to talk to you is perceived by them as disrespectful.

KEY 4: Don't pile on a bunch of criticisms. Stick to the original topic of discussion. Pulling up unrelated and unresolved hurt feelings from the past and introducing them into a new conflict only confuses matters.

KEY 5: Try a communication style called "shared meaning." Here's how it works:

You're bugged that you can't go out with your friends on Friday night, so you approach Mom and Dad and say, "Could we please talk about this? I'd like you to hear my side."

Once they agree to hear you out, you explain your point of view (which you've thought through ahead of time) without being interrupted.

Next, Mom and Dad repeat what they heard you say.

You then clarify or confirm what they said, ensuring that your thoughts and feelings have been heard accurately.

The process continues with their sharing their point of view and your listening and repeating what they said.

The goal of shared meaning is to be heard accurately. And once you've had a chance to state your case and listen to theirs, the foundation is set for communication and for a fair solution to what's bugging you.

Day 28: Family Fights

How to Avoid Sibling Homicide

Peacemakers who sow in peace raise a harvest of righteousness (James 3:18).

"Why do I get blamed for everything?" Gina screamed from the top of her lungs.

Her mom crossed her arms and locked eyes with the 17-year-old. "Watch your tone, young lady," she said in a low, stern voice. "You're not always blamed, but you are the oldest in this family—and you know better. I want you to set a good example."

Suddenly, Gina's little brother, who had taken cover behind their mom, secretly got Gina's attention, stuck out his tongue, then grinned from ear to ear.

"Did you see that?" Gina gasped. "The little jerk is doing it again."

"Doing what, Gina?" her mom responded. "He's just standing here—trying to avoid getting clobbered by you."

Gina gasped. Just before slamming her bedroom door, she launched one last missile: "Not only is he treated better, but you and Dad let him get away with murder."

Once inside her room, Gina flopped onto her bed and buried her face into her pillow.

Why do I have to put up with this garbage, she thought. *I get abso-*

lutely no privacy and no respect for my stuff. And that slimy little maggot! He listens in on my phone conversations and has no idea how to keep a secret.

Gina was convinced that her parents conceived her brother just to spy on her. *He's like a miniature double agent, she told herself. Just when I thought I could trust him, he tells Mom what I did last week—and I get grounded for the next three years. And as Mom pronounces punishment, that ever-so-faint smile plays across the little jerks lips. Oh, if only I could smack that smile off his lips just once!*

Think About It! **Fighting with brothers and sisters is a fact of family life you just can't escape.** Yet it's important to know that your relationship with your brothers and sisters will have a direct effect on your relationship with your mother and father. According to popular youth speaker Ken Davis, few things can cause a parent to become a raving maniac quicker than constant bickering and fighting.

"If you learn to fight with your brothers and sisters less frequently, you'll notice a change in your parents," Ken often tells teens. "The glassy gaze and the dark circles beneath their eyes will disappear. Their voices will become much quieter, and they won't foam at the mouth as often."[2]

But what can you do to save your sanity and bring peace to the home front?

Explore these scriptures:

Feed Your Face

Ps. 133

Matt. 5:1-12

Titus 3:1-11

Have a time-out period. If you're ticked at your little brother or sister and are on the verge of slugging him or her between the eyes, step back, take a deep breath, and give yourself time to calm down.

Avoid getting a bitterness burn. Bitterness hurts you far more than it hurts others. Here's how the danger of an unforgiving heart can be described: It's like a hot coal. The longer and tighter it is held, the deeper the burn. Like a hot coal, bitterness too will leave a scar that even time cannot erase.

Forgive—then forgive again. Think of all the ways you feel you have been wronged by your brother or sister; then work toward genuine forgiveness. But first understand that forgiveness is not (a) denying that you've been hurt, (b) explaining away the wrong action someone has brought against you, or (c) trying to understand why a person has acted a certain way. Genuine forgiveness involves consciously choosing to release the hurt someone has caused—and continuing to love that person. Can you get to this point with the family member who has wronged you?

Fight your own battles. Don't report every little disagreement to Mom and Dad. Sit down with the one who, you feel, wronged you and figure out how to settle the conflict on your own. And as you confront your sibling, avoid assigning fault. Instead, concentrate on finding a solution to your problem.

Fight fair. Fighting fair means never keeping score or popping off with a statement like "This is the billionth time I've forgiven you, and I refuse to do it anymore." Even if you'd love to tear the lips right off your little brother, God wants you to forgive him. After all, Christ doesn't put limits on His love for you.

---

1. Americans for Divorce Reform, <http://www.divorcereform.org/rates.html> accessed July 22, 2007.

---

2. Reprinted from *How to Live with Your Parents Without Losing Your Mind.* © 1988 by Zondervan Publishing House.